RUN

Brian Tobin's Quest for a Second Term

By Doug Letto

RUN

Brian Tobin's Quest for a Second Term

By Doug Letto

Blue Hill Publishing
Paradise, Newfoundland
1999

Cover Design: Bruce Bourque
Cover Photo: Greg Locke
Author Photo: Ty Evans

Printed by:
Robinson-Blackmore Printing and Publishing
St. John's, Newfoundland, Canada

∞ Printed on acid-free paper

Published by: Blue Hill Publishing
P.O. Box 18 — Site 14 — RR #2
Paradise, Newfoundland, Canada
A1L 1C2

Canadian Cataloguing in Publication Data

Letto, Douglas Mervyn, 1958-

Run

1st ed.

Includes index.

ISBN 0-9684326-1-1

1. Tobin, Brian, 1954- 2. Politicians — Newfoundland — 20th century. 3. Newfoundland. House of Assembly — Elections, 1999. I. Title.

FC2177.1.T62L47 1999 971.8'04'092 C99-950229-8
F1123.L47 1999

To my family

Bob Parsons
19A Holbrook Ave
St. John's, NL
A1E 2Y2

Table of Contents

Prologue

Brian Tobin was a man in a hurry in 1998. He began thinking about an election in the late spring, and commenced to put things in order should he need to call a snap vote. The budget was out of the way in the spring, changes were made to the Elections Act just before the legislature closed in June, and members had their pictures taken just in case the party needed to get the printing presses going for production of election materials.

Tobin didn't require a new mandate in 1998, he was only halfway through his term. But his political radar was picking up signs of trouble - thousands of provincial public servants, including nurses, wanted to emerge from a near decade of frozen wages. Where would the money come from? The TAGS fisheries compensation program was ending, and people would get their last cheques in late fall or early winter. Add to that, the giant nickel discovery at Voisey's Bay, Labrador was not going to be developed quickly.

Brian Tobin says the moment he starts thinking about an election, the matter takes on a life of its own. That certainly was the case in the summer of 1998.

This book is about Brian Tobin's quest for a second term, a search that ended in victory for his Liberal Party on February 9, 1999.

Brian Tobin is not the only character in this book. But he is the central character, as he has been since his return to Newfoundland from federal politics in January 1996. This book traces the story from the "summer tour" of 1998, the 'dry-run' election as some have called it. You will meet many of the politicians; all of them played a role in a Brian Tobin-led drama.

Brian Tobin was the subject of much intense questioning as he made his quest for a new mandate. Many people believed his 'real' motives were not the leadership issues he defined at the start of the campaign, but rather, a desire to get an election out of the way to avoid getting caught campaigning in a future political storm. And then, there was his perceived interest in succeeding Jean Chretien as leader of the federal Liberals. An electoral victory would give Tobin five good years to wait for his chance.

This book was made possible because of the co-operation of many of the participants in the election. I also kept an election diary, parts of which will be quoted in this book.

Chapter 1

Pre-Election

Brian Tobin sat back in the leather bound chair behind the Premier's desk on the eighth floor of Confederation Building. The office is a politically correct blend of native art, Newfoundland-inspired paintings, a Newfoundland schooner, the Canadian and Newfoundland flags, and an oil painting of the Montreal rally organized by Tobin in the days leading up to the Quebec referendum in 1995. The painting was commissioned by the brother of Bob Rae, the former NDP Premier of Ontario. Brian Tobin treasures it as a gift. On the opposite wall is a Newfoundland painting in three parts by Jim Miller. The focus is a lonely fisherman in a small boat on the crest of a wave. It is one of Brian Tobin's favourites, summing up the job he has held since returning from Ottawa as fisheries minister in early 1996. Pointing to the Miller painting, he puts the lone sailor's situation in his own perspective: "is he riding the wave or will he be swamped by it?" With a wave of his hand, Tobin concludes "that's what this job feels like."

Outside, a cold December chill gripped St. John's in a knot. Much, perhaps, like the chill Tobin and his caucus had endured for the past couple of days. He was grappling with what to do about his Minister of Municipal and Provincial Affairs, Art Reid. Two days earlier, Reid brought the afternoon legislative session to a standstill with remarks that had since been played and replayed on radio and television. In the midst of debate, Reid insulted Conservative MHA Sheila Osborne, and it seemed, much of Newfoundland and Labrador, with a declaration that "she go back to the kitchen where she came from."

I had just finished a television interview with the Premier for a segment I was doing on the evening news about Tobin's handling of the "kitchen affair". In the interview, he underlined how improper and uncalled for, Reid's remarks had been. He said Reid had apologized and that would be the end of the matter. Tobin left one small opening for Reid's departure though — he noted Reid would stay unless the minister decided otherwise.

The conversation then turned to cabinet-making. Tobin led the discussion, making the point that Premiers should not give advance warning about such shuffles. All that serves to do he related, is make everyone in caucus anxious, and lead to expectations that cannot possibly be filled, since there are always more MHA's than there are cabinet posts. It was around four o'clock when the cameraman and myself left Tobin's office.

The next morning Tobin struck early and shuffled his cabinet. Art Reid was out of the cabinet and out of sight in his Carbonear constituency. Brian Tobin was not to be out-scooped on his big story.

Brian Tobin has few equals in the political profession in Newfoundland. He is calculating and that means he is always attempting to 'read' a given situation. In a debate, that gives him the room to trump an opposition speaker and be seen as a champion. In a wider political debate about an important question of public policy, it gives Tobin the opportunity to come out on the 'right' side of the debate, and thereby become the politician who frames the public discussion that follows. He drags a committee of Newfoundland party leaders to Ottawa on the Term 17 question for constitutional change in education, and he brings them there to argue for a program to replace the TAGS program for fisheries compensation. The Opposition leaders go because Tobin gives them no choice. And they are there on his terms, the meetings arranged by Tobin and the cadre of connections he established over 16 years in federal politics.

And so it is with elections. Tobin, like the deft hockey player carrying the puck, looking for the opening to go all the way to score the game-winning goal. One of his confidantes regards Tobin as the best intelligence gatherer of any politician in Canada. The Premier has a long list of contacts, not only in Newfoundland, but across the country. This is the result of his decade and a half in federal politics and nearly four years as Premier. People around Tobin regard his political antennae as being acute, especially when he is contemplating the timing for an election. "He was toying with people, putting the idea out there, and seeing what the feedback would be," one Liberal said of Tobin's manoueverings in the summer of 1998. "Brian wanted us to be ready for an election, he is very keen to see an opportunity." Wanting an election is one matter, but calling it at the right time is quite another. That is the quest Tobin set himself on as the spring legislative session concluded in June 1998.

An election was very much on Tobin's mind that summer. Only two-and-a-half years into the job, Tobin was itching for some action. Talks on developing the Voisey's Bay nickel deposit in Labrador were going nowhere. INCO, hurting because of slumping nickel prices, which led to losses and slumping share prices, wanted out of its commitment to build a $1.3-billion dollar smelter at the site of the former World War II naval base at Argentia, in Placentia Bay. The company would build a mine in Labrador, but it wanted to ship the nickel outside Newfoundland for processing. Tobin and the government said no and talks broke off. This was just the type of issue to take to the public, or was it?

Tobin himself had concluded "the standoff" with INCO was enough of an issue to go to the electorate. But he was also mindful it had only been thirty months since his first election in February 1996. That fact would have to be weighed against his claim that INCO was posturing, and would only take Newfoundland seriously after his government had a new mandate, or another party was elected. "You need to remove the notion from the mind of the other side that there may be a change of policy, that the government will do a deal to hold up in the window of an election campaign."

Liberal polling showed strong support for the government's position. But that was about it. One Liberal complained the support "ran a mile wide and an inch deep." The government, if it were to push the Voisey's issue as an election call, would run out of things to talk about real fast.

Tobin began to warm up the election machine in June. He appointed four cabinet ministers — Beaton Tulk, Kevin Aylward, Sandra Kelly and Ernest McLean — to a committee of ministers to review government's approach to outdoors issues. This was largely a response to the claims asserted by some groups that the government planned to allow outfitters and others to own lakes and ponds. That, it was argued, would interfere with the general population's long-standing right to go into the woods and fish. Chair Beaton Tulk tried a preemptive strike on that assertion. "We will not privatize the outdoors," he told reporters.

Cabinet met in Stephenville in mid-July, a meeting that coincided with the Stephenville Festival. Brian Tobin and the local MHA — Kevin Aylward, turned the sod for a new 1400-seat arena to be used for the coming Canada Winter Games. Six days later, on July 23, Brian Tobin was in Gander with Newfoundlander Craig Dobbin, chairman and CEO of Canadian Helicopters. Dobbin had set up a new company, Newfoundland Bonding and Composites, to build components for the aerospace industry. Newfoundland put up $9.5 million of the $20.5 million to get the company started. The first contract would be one to manufacture "skin panels" for the new Cormorant helicopters ordered by Canada's Department of National Defence. MHA Sandra Kelly welcomed the 250 jobs the company forecasted it would average over the coming six years; Brian Tobin felt Newfoundland had found an important place in the expanding aerospace industry.

Tobin continued to hog the spotlight for the rest of July. A day after the Gander announcement, he was in St. Lawrence, with a promise of $10 million to construct a new wharf should the St. Lawrence fluorspar mine come back in operation. The government's contribution was tied to the results of new drilling taking place, and to efforts by the new owners to come up with $38.5 million in private financing. Tobin, the local MHA Judy Foote and Mines Minister Chuck Furey attended the announcement, which was really nothing more than a conditional promise to help. A year later, the new owners had drilled only some of the core samples they needed in order to prove feasibility, and were looking to investors to come up with more money for the drilling program.

Brian Tobin's "provincial tour" was intended to be a mixture of positive announcements and a chance for "the boss" to find out for himself the political temperature of the various districts. He took a breather from the tour on July 27th and attended business in St. John's. But even while there, Tobin cranked up the information flow. The province's credit rating had been upgraded by the Dominion Bond Rating Service, the first time in 25 years this had happened, Tobin reported in a statement. He viewed the upgrading as a vindication of the budget decisions his government had taken. The real proof was the gains in employment, all of it signaling Newfoundland "has turned a significant corner."

That evening, Tobin released a statement on the failure of talks between Newfoundland and INCO regarding the proposed Voisey's Bay nickel development. INCO had decided it could not commit to the smelter-refinery complex it agreed to in November 1996. "Our bottom line has not changed — no smelter/refinery — no mill/mine," Tobin said in a statement, adding that Newfoundland's own analysis indicated such a development was feasible. This though, was not a political battle. INCO could not be pushed into doing something it said it could not afford, at least not yet. Tobin could only state the province's bottom line — that the people and government "are willing to wait for a project that provides full and fair benefits."

The next day, Tobin toured the Northern Peninsula with Mines and Energy Minister Chuck Furey. Few doubted Furey's chance of being reelected, but just in case, Tobin was there for marquis appeal. They stopped in Black Duck Cove to announce 100 people would work at a renovated shrimp and crab processing plant. Tobin talked about "a brighter future for the people" from an area devastated by the collapse of groundfish stocks. Furey called it a "win-win situation". Later, they stopped off at Cow Head in Gros Morne National Park. Former Cow Head resident Alphonse Hutchings announced plans for a 52-room, five-star resort, complete with 18-hole golf course and indoor beach swimming pool. Tobin called it "an outstanding economic boost" and Furey gushed about the "world-class facility" about to be built.

While the pundits and politicians speculated about an election call, Tobin retired for a few days from the front pages. In early August though, he was back in form. Attending the Premier's Conference in

Saskatoon, Tobin announced that he and Nova Scotia Premier Russell MacLellan had agreed to send their dispute over the offshore boundary between Cape Breton Island and Newfoundland to arbitration. Tobin noted Newfoundland's and Nova Scotia's "close, effective, and productive relationship", and suggested he did not want a boundary dispute to cause bad feelings and impair offshore oil exploration, since "the highly prospective area has the potential to generate jobs and royalties for both provinces."

Tobin admits his summer tour was part of a plan to determine first-hand if the province was ready for an election. But he also argues summer travel is an important part of an elected official's life. He says that was a lesson imparted by Don Jamieson, Newfoundland's representative in the federal cabinet in Pierre Trudeau's 1970's governments. Tobin had served for a time as Jamieson's executive assistant, before successfully running for federal office himself in 1980. "Don said that an awful lot of people in his time in Ottawa got caught up in the Ottawa games, were spectacular successes in their first term, they got noticed," says Tobin. "The trouble is they never got reelected."

On August 7th, Statistics Canada reported Newfoundland's unemployment rate at 17.4 percent, a drop of one full percentage point from the same month in 1997. Tobin and the government have a team of economists in the Newfoundland Statistics Agency to analyze employment and other economic data, and good news is their moment to shine. Tobin spared no effort in publicizing the new numbers. "There were 7,600 more jobs in July than there were a year earlier" he reported, and so no one could misunderstand the significance of the news, "only one other province, Alberta, recorded a stronger increase in employment." Tobin went on to note that the January to July employment numbers were the best in nearly a decade; retail trade had grown over the same period last year; the value of manufacturing shipments was up by 14 percent, and iron ore production was up by 5.6 percent. In non-election times, the minister of employment makes these announcements. In the summer of 1998, with an election on Tobin's mind, this was the material for announcements by the Premier.

The Conservatives watched the gathering election clouds with both a sense of apprehension and anticipation. The party didn't have a policy document together and it did not have the funds to finance an election campaign. But the Conservatives had a new leader, and although Ed Byrne had been in the job just a few months, he was anxious to prove he belonged in the same ring as Brian Tobin.

In early August, as Tobin continued his tour, Byrne summoned a group of people to write a policy document for the expected election campaign. His chief of staff, Bruce Peckford, co-chaired the policy group along with Ray Andrews, a former provincial deputy minister of fisheries and former assistant to John Crosbie. A group with impeccable Conservative credentials rounded out the list — former Newfoundland and Labrador Hydro chair Cyril Abery; former deputy minister of justice Ron Penney; former party president, ex-deputy minister of education and one-time teachers association president Lorne Wheeler; and St. John's lawyer Valerie Marshall.

Certain the election was coming, Byrne and the group got down to the task of writing policy. Although the policy would eventually have to be approved by caucus, it was necessary to have it in as concise a form as possible. The party had consulted with people in various regions through the early summer, and they were assisted in their task by unnamed civil servants who provided information about government policy and the shape of various programs. Says Ed Byrne, "they shall remain unnamed. [They] gave us significant insight into what was happening inside Tobin's administration." Through the regional policy group and the civil servants, a policy document began to emerge that covered the major social areas of health and education, as well as the resource areas of fisheries and mines and energy. The policy group met nightly through the end of August, and Byrne hired a writer to put the policy ideas into a document.

Byrne prides himself on his ability to organize. Along with the policy work, he had visited dozens of communities through the summer of 1998. His main job was to make sure district associations became active, and to recruit candidates for the anticipated election. He had also put a "creative team" in place after becoming party leader.

The creative team's job was to identify public issues through polling, and determine how people viewed the party and the leader. Thirty-two year old Craig Tucker headed the group. With a degree in commerce and a major in marketing, Tucker had already worked on 14 district and leadership campaigns. The group had an opinion poll carried out and it pointed to health and education as the major issues. The poll also told Tucker and his group a number of things about Ed Byrne and Brian Tobin. For starters, the public viewed Byrne as "maybe too young to be Premier", while Tobin was viewed as a "seasoned veteran." They also found out that Tobin had strong support from female voters, while Byrne resonated more with young voters and those generally "disillusioned with the Liberal government." Those findings persuaded Tucker and his group to cast Ed Byrne as a team player, rather than focus on leadership. "When we matched up [Tobin and Byrne] head-to-head, we were concerned," says Tucker. The issue with the Conservative campaign — "do we play the team approach, [or] do we play the individual approach?"

The results of that poll, and a subsequent one in the fall, confirmed the health and education issues as priorities for the public. And it also confirmed that the Conservative advertising campaign in the election should focus on the team rather than Ed Byrne as leader. The strategy was in place, even if the party did not yet have the money to make it work.

On August 19, Tobin was again making an announcement. This time it had to do with a $10 million dollar resort planned for Deer Lake. This was private sector funds, and Tobin announced it "underscores international business confidence in the tourism future of Newfoundland and Labrador." It was not only jobs that would result from this project, according to Tobin, the builders share "in the vision of the 'new' Newfoundland and Labrador, and tourism is a big part of that vision."

The West Coast summer weather, the fact that Tobin and several of his ministers held seats in the region, and that the area afforded province-wide media coverage without the oppressive naysayers of St. John's, all contributed to a comfortable setting for Tobin and his ministers. On August 21, he was in Corner Brook announcing a $1.2

million grant for the privately-owned Blomidon Golf and Country Club. Again tourism was the focus, and Tobin quoted from a 1995 provincial study that showed "the tourism golf product in Newfoundland and Labrador was seriously underdeveloped."

On August 31st, Tobin gave the clearest signal yet than he wanted to preserve the option of calling an election. Joined by Energy Minister Chuck Furey, Newfoundland and Labrador Hydro President and CEO Bill Wells, and Jim Thistle, the chief negotiator on the Churchill Falls Project, Tobin announced all small hydro projects would be suspended until a full energy policy review was completed. The Northwest and Southwest River projects were especially controversial, as salmon conservation groups claimed the developments would interfere with the rebuilding of salmon stocks. The government also thought it necessary to tell the public the review would not raise the troublesome issue of privatizing Newfoundland and Labrador Hydro , and underlined Hydro would not be owned "by anyone other than the people of the province." This valuable lesson had been learned by the Clyde Wells government in the early 1990's. After spending millions on feasibility studies and other projects associated with taking Hydro private, the government gave up the privatization bid in the face of stiff public opposition. That concern emanated from the open line shows, the opposition parties, and the general public. Brian Tobin was not about to become embroiled in the same kind of politically destructive controversy.

Inside the Liberal caucus, people had been told to be ready in case Tobin called an election. Some of the necessary groundwork for an election had already been done. Pictures that Liberals could use in election advertising, had been taken when the House broke in June for the summer vacation. As August came in, some MHA's were talking about the need for a "solid mandate" to make sure there was no repeat of the Churchill Falls deal with INCO. Other Liberal insiders talked of Tobin "looking for an issue to go to the polls." Tobin had also been to Quebec to do an intensive French Immersion program, proof he still coveted the federal leadership should Jean Chretien step aside.

Yet, it was Newfoundland politics that interested Liberal politicians in St. John's, and it was the Voisey's Bay issue that consumed them. One Liberal insider, who had the comfort of viewing the goings-on from the sidelines, felt "by this time next year, Tobin will be there (to the polls) and back." But he noted Tobin's caution about elections, how even when Tobin returned from Ottawa in 1996 to take Clyde Wells' job, he had "poll after poll done, to ensure he had it." Tobin was not a guy who would call a vote without being sure. Clyde Wells on the other hand called his second election without relying heavily on the polls. "With Clyde Wells, polling would have been the third or fourth thing to be done. He would have called the election on the issues" according to a Liberal who has served in both governments. But Tobin would combine the issues with accurate polling "so he has a decent read of the political landscape."

Liberal cabinet ministers and others in the caucus had been told by Tobin to be ready in case he called a snap vote for August or September of 1998. Kevin Aylward, the not-yet-40 minister of Forestry and Agriculture, would spend most of the summer in his district of Stephenville East. While his family vacationed in two area parks, Aylward pounded the trail in the district, attending socials and sniffing the political air. His concern was not only what people thought of the government, but more important before an election, who might be in a position to challenge him for the Liberal nomination, and past that, who might come forward for the other parties.

Fisheries and Aquaculture Minister John Efford spends as much of his free time as possible in the summer on his boat. Like Aylward, Efford was elected in the 1985 election. He and his campaign workers also had to contend with the election talk. When Brian Tobin told Efford "I haven't made up my mind yet," Efford went back to plying the waters of Conception Bay. He told his supporters not to worry, with a full campaign chest, and 250 workers to call on, the Port de Grave Liberals would be ready whenever the election was called.

All the while, politicians and their advisors started mapping out who would face off against whom. Some Liberals talked about Loyola Sullivan jumping from the Conservatives to their side. They speculated Mount Pearl Mayor Dave Denine would run for the Liberals against Tory Harvey Hodder. Sean Hanrahan might run against

New Democrat leader Jack Harris in Signal Hill-Quidi Vidi. Lynn Verge, although "relaxed and happy with her life," might decide to run in Humber East. That rumour held the most fear for the Liberals, since Verge was still held in high regard by the public, and people remembered she had defeated Clyde Wells in his quest for a seat in the Liberal victory in 1989. Only when Eddy Joyce stepped down in Bay of Islands, could Wells run in a by-election and take a seat in the legislature.

By this time, the Conservatives had twenty candidates nominated. Liberal MHA's were checking out the political landscape in their districts, and more important for some of the Liberal incumbents, potential competitors were doing the same thing. There were some signs of trouble for sitting government MHA's. 700 new Liberals had signed cards in Don Whalen's district of Harbour Main-Whitbourne. He would face a challenge for the nomination from Wanda Dawe, a rematch of 1996. In Lapoile, 1000 Liberals signed cards, a sign that incumbent Bill Ramsey would face a challenge. The same kind of activity was happening in Lewisporte where Melvin Penney held the seat since the Liberals came to power in 1989.

As August unfolded, Liberals, even the cautious ones, felt Tobin was moving closer to calling an election. One said Tobin was "ready to pull the plug" on the Voisey's Bay issue, and felt certain Newfoundlanders would endorse his position, as they had done nearly two decades earlier with Brian Peckford on the offshore. It was felt Tobin's summer trip around the province "gave him the confidence" to call a vote. Liberals were even anticipating how to react to suggestions Tobin wanted a quick vote in order to be ready for a run at the Liberal leadership in the event Chretien left office. "It would not be such a bad thing" one suggested, adding Newfoundlanders might like to see one of their own become Prime Minister.

The summer-long parade of announcements fit in with a strategy Brian Tobin has perfected since he became a federal cabinet minister in the Liberal victory of 1993. His pan-Newfoundland and Labrador trip in July and August 1998 put that strategy into play. "He believes totally that you create the issue, set the agenda, that's his mantra," said one of his colleagues in relation to all those press conferences, appearances and announcements. All the time, Tobin was searching for an opening to call a vote. "Brian always looks for the opportunity to do things," says one who knows him well. "He's one of the people I know who loves elections, he loves shaking hands, he loves the parry and thrust of being in with people."

Inside the Liberal caucus, ministers and others were seized with the prospect of an election call. One minister called the experience "gut-wrenching," as the wait dragged out over several weeks. The veteran politicians screwed up their courage and pronounced themselves ready for a campaign, but several of the first-term Liberal MHA's were more reticent. It was not just that they wanted a second term to qualify for a pension, but many looked at the long list of one-term MHA's and did not relish the thought of joining them.

Liberal members who wanted a summer campaign felt they could take on INCO over Voisey's Bay because "the company had laid down a position we would not be able to tolerate." The tentative agreement on the Churchill Falls deal was felt by the summer campaign proponents to be another good reason to take Newfoundlanders to the polls early.

Jack Harris has been a member of the Newfoundland legislature since he was elected in a by-election, to replace Conservative Shannie Duff in the old district of St. John's East in December 1990. A 50-year old lawyer, and briefly, New Democrat Member of Parliament for St. John's East, Harris did not believe Tobin would want to go to the polls in 1998. "There was no reason to call an election," he says. "I couldn't imagine him concocting one over the summer." Harris concluded Tobin's summer tour "didn't have a campaign rhythm about it. It did not have a 'feel-good' feel about it." Yet, Harris had paid some attention to Tobin's anxiety just before the legislature closed in June 1998. Changes were made to the Elections Act, "and I know Tobin was very interested in having the changes brought in."

Harris had his own reasons for not wanting a vote in the late summer. "1998 was not my best year," he says, recalling his failed bid for the mayoralty of St. John's in the previous fall. In a heated battle with the eventual winner, Andy Wells, Harris was involved in a month-long recount. Although he had committed to staying with the New Democrats, even if he won the city's top job, Harris said some party members were asking tough questions. "How could he go back to the party if he was Mayor of St. John's," he recalls some people asking. Others were more direct, feeling Harris had sold out his party for the job as mayor.

Jack Harris spent most of 1998 attempting to convince New Democrats he was serious about continuing to lead the party. He went to Corner Brook in June to speak to the CUPE convention, and he spoke to other groups. In a case like his, Harris recalls, "you take every opportunity you had. You knew it was an issue. You let people know your commitment is to the party and to the future." Harris felt Brian Tobin would call a vote for the spring of 1999 and wanted his party ready for that.

But not everyone in the NDP felt Tobin would call a vote that soon, so Harris had to push hard for a party convention in the fall of 1998. A convention would serve the dual purpose of creating a higher public profile for the party, and it would persuade party members Harris was committed to leading the NDP into the next election. Harris was pleased with the overall press coverage of the convention, but a little miffed that former leader Peter Fenwick had written a column in *The Telegram* suggesting the New Democrats were not the party they used to be.

Election speculation reached near fever-pitch at the end of August. "I thought it was coming" said a Liberal who felt he would have no trouble retaining his seat. Another said of Tobin and his plans, "I thought his mind was nearly made up." But Tobin, who had spent much of the summer on the road in Newfoundland and Labrador, talking issues and making announcements, backed off on an election call. "There was a sudden shift," is how one powerful Liberal saw things. "For whatever reason, he suddenly changed his mind. Friday, he was all prepared, almost ready to go. He was thinking about the campaign and this sort of thing. Monday, he decided 'no', we're not having an election."

Why had Tobin changed his mind, when he had so deliberately spent an entire summer gearing up the troops, readying the election machinery, and creating announcement after announcement? Some of those closest to him say the answer may lie in his faith in the polls and his own political instincts, honed over twenty years in federal and political politics.

Tobin had chosen the issues should he have called a snap vote in the late summer. He would ask the entire province to back his position that INCO must live up to its earlier promise to build a smelter at Argentia to process nickel from Voisey's Bay. INCO would not get away with breaking off talks on the issue in the job-starved province, in order to pressure Newfoundland to bend to the company's request to have unprocessed ore shipped out of Labrador. Tobin's second issue would be the agreement-in-principle with Quebec to increase compensation to Newfoundland from the infamous Churchill Falls hydro deal, and at the same time, to substantially increase power production at that site and to develop new hydro power from the Lower Churchill. In some ways, the Churchill Falls issue resonated best for Liberals. More than thirty years after Smallwood gave BRINCO the right to develop and own Labrador resources, including Churchill Falls, here was a chance for a new Liberal government headed by a younger generation, to make a kind of political restitution to the people who had suffered through twenty-three years of a deal that had cost Newfoundland tens of billions of dollars. One Liberal summed it up — here was the chance "to deal with the Quebec issue and fix the history."

As Tobin read the political tea leaves in late August, he found signs of concern that he was unable to alter. First was his caucus. Many would only reluctantly have given their blessing to an election. They were concerned about explaining to the public the need for an election in a government that had only been elected two-and-a-half years earlier. Caucus members reported "an unsettling feeling. What if you go door-to-door and people ask you 'why are you calling an election', and you don't have an answer for them?" The second factor, perhaps one that weighed more heavily, was the indifference Tobin and the Liberals detected on the part of the public to their planned Voisey's Bay-Churchill Falls offensive. "If there had been some question in the public about Voisey's Bay," Tobin would have been able to conduct an election with ease, even a campaign in the middle of his mandate. But said one insider, "because there was overwhelming support for it, the argument was why have an election when everyone is onside on this issue."

Liberals had a recent example to cite when discussion inside the cabinet and caucus intensified on the possibility of an election call. Everyone remembered David Peterson in Ontario in 1991. Just over two years into his mandate, Peterson called a snap vote to take advantage of his high standing in the polls. Liberals and just about everyone else got the shock of their lives when Ontario voters turned Peterson out of office and replaced him with Bob Rae and the New Democrats. "The Peterson example in Ontario" was the fodder for discussion in the Newfoundland Liberal Party, and the fact Peterson "got trounced" by taking Ontario voters for granted, did not leave the Newfoundland caucus with a comfortable feeling.

But it was not just the lukewarm response in the public that prompted the Premier to hesitate. Several Liberal MHA's, a couple of them cabinet ministers, were worried about winning their districts. Bill Ramsey in Lapoile already knew he would have competition for the party nomination; Melvin Penney in Lewisporte was facing the same prospect. In Gander, Tourism Minister Sandra Kelly was viewed as a weak minister. She snagged the party nomination practically by default in the February 1996 election when her Liberal opponent — then MHA Gary Vey — was charged with indecent assault. (The case went to trial; Vey was aquitted in December 1996, ten months after the election). In St. John's Centre, Health Minister Joan Marie Aylward was about to face Conservative Paul Brown who came to within 200 votes of Aylward in the 1996 election. In the interim, Brown served as a 'shadow member', helping constituents with problems and generally being an advocate. And in Lake Melville, Government Services Minister Ernie McLean was going to be challenged for the party nomination.

Tobin finally made a public statement on the first of September while he was on business in Happy Valley-Goose Bay. There would be no election in 1998. Liberals who did not want an election felt relief. Tobin did not say why he had geared toward an election and then backed off, but a Liberal said it came down to the realization that the public was unwilling to take seriously that there was a need for an election so soon. Tobin was not prepared to take the risk, as Peterson had done in Ontario earlier in the decade. Said one Liberal, "when you get into the campaign, you have to be able to sustain it for three or four weeks. You not only have to have the issues lined up, they have to have some substance to them."

But even as Tobin said there would be no election in the fall of 1998, his mind was racing about the next appropriate and right moment. He said "it was very much in my mind to clear the decks as quickly as possible" in the context of the Voisey's Bay and Churchill Falls negotiations.

Chapter 2

The Conservatives

Ed Byrne had lots on his mind as his car sped down the Southern Shore highway on a sunny day in October 1998. He was on a mission to persuade a respected former Conservative politician to offer him some help in the lead-up to a provincial election. Brian Tobin might have backed off from a September vote, but everyone, including Byrne, had to see that "dry run" as fair warning that Tobin would likely call a vote for sometime in 1999. Byrne was on his way to have another try at convincing Loyola Hearn to step back into an active role in the Conservative Party.

Loyola Hearn left provincial politics when Clyde Wells called the spring election in 1993. After fourteen years representing St. Mary's — The Capes, Hearn wanted out of political life. He went back to the field he had left for politics — education. Private colleges spread their campuses throughout the province in the early 1990's, spurred by the federal retraining money offered to the fishing industry as a result of the groundfish moratorium. Keyin Technical College, later to become Keycorp, was in on this growth. The Southern Shore, with its dependence on the fishery, was seen as a natural place to expand. Loyola Hearn, now out of politics, saw this as a golden opportunity to live and work in his hometown of Renews.

Ed Byrne knew Hearn would not be an easy sell. But as the two men sat over tea in Hearn's home, Byrne appealed to the man who had been such a big help to him when he first ran in Kilbride district. In that election, Hearn came out to Kilbride to help sway voters who had once lived on the Southern Shore. Ed Byrne now was in a position to hire Hearn. His chief of staff, Bruce Peckford, had left for the private sector. Hearn's organizational skills would be a big asset to the new Conservative leader, and so would his people skills. "He knows how to deal with people," says Byrne, "and people have respect for him." A week later, Hearn dropped into Ed Byrne's house, and over another cup of tea, worked out a plan for the former member of St. Mary's — The Capes to assume the position as Ed Byrne's chief of staff. It was agreed Hearn would start in the job just after Christmas.

Ed Byrne might not have admitted it in public, but he was dealing with his own crisis in the fall of 1998. He had assumed the Conservative leadership uncontested, after interim leader Loyola Sullivan did his own read of the Newfoundland political landscape and the Conservative party, and decided he would not continue in the job. Byrne had not intended to go for the leader's job. Indeed, everyone but Byrne seemed to be in the running, as speculation mounted that Loyola Sullivan would not stay. Baie Verte MHA Paul Shelley took a look, so did John Ottenheimer of St. John's East. Bay Roberts lawyer and long-time Conservative Doug Moores actually announced his candidacy on a Friday morning. By Monday, Moores had backed out, saying he had done so on the advice of his doctor. Ed Byrne had given some early consideration to the leadership, but backed off, saying it was the wrong time to devote so much effort to the job given that he and his wife Bernie, were raising two young children. With Shelley and Ottenheimer out of the running, people went back to Byrne again. This time he said yes. One of his close associates, Kim Puddister, says "he was the last one who thought he would be leader. He was recruited. I only wish now that we probably had a leadership race for people to see that, to counter the impression he was a leader by default".

Kim Puddister had known Ed Byrne from his days as a student leader at Memorial University, and his early involvement in the Conservative Party. He was thorough and he was an expert at organization. Says Puddister, "we had a policy team in place two or three months after Ed became leader". Byrne visited the districts, made sure district associations were reactivated, organized the provincial Conservative Party apparatus, and generally got people working toward the next election.

But the fact that Ed Byrne had come to the job reluctantly and that he got the job without any opposition, left party members and many in the public feeling lukewarm. And not only that, Byrne was operating in the considerable shadow cast by Premier Brian Tobin. "Every time you turned on the TV, Tobin was there and people were saying he's smooth," complained one Conservative, who is close to Byrne. "We had to spend the first while saying, 'look, Tobin is not the Messiah'."

And Byrne had his own enemies in the Conservative Party. No one would forget the interview he and Roger Fitzgerald gave to *Here & Now* just after the 1996 election, when Brian Tobin reduced the Conservatives under Lynn Verge to ten seats. Verge had lost her own seat in Humber East, and was considering asking for a recount. Byrne and Fitzgerald, just two of a substantial number of Conservatives who objected to Verge's style of leadership, called for her to step aside and allow the party to move on. Their fear was that Verge would attempt to stay on as leader, despite her failure in the general election.

That feud had its beginnings in the 1989 leadership campaign to find a successor to the then-departing Premier, Brian Peckford. Ed Byrne was in the Len Simms camp and Lynn Verge was a strong supporter of the eventual winner, Tom Rideout. Simms' people felt Rideout was given an unfair head start for the leadership by no one less than Brian Peckford himself. Rideout hired Conservative leadership guru John Laschinger, the man who organized Brian Peckford's successful run at the leadership ten years earlier in 1979. Rideout won the race, but the Conservative political machine that had tasted power for seventeen years, ran out of luck. Part of it was disorganization, partly a strong showing put on by Clyde Wells and the Liberals, partly that people had grown tired of the Conservatives, but just as important, the Conservatives had become arrogant and contemptuous of the public during the latter Peckford years. Rideout, Simms, Verge, Sullivan, and now Ed Byrne would be left to try and pick up the pieces and restore the Conservative Party to political glory by taking on the government.

Conservatives, including Ed Byrne, claim the feud between he and Lynn Verge is over. Yet, they discuss few details about how the matter was resolved. "You'd have to be hurt," says one confidant of both Bryne and Verge, about the comments made in the 1996 television interview by Byrne and Fitzgerald. "But I don't think she puts as much into the television interview as the people around her." For his part, Byrne says he and Verge "did what we had to do" in settling the dispute. "I've had some regrets in politics, that was one of them," he says. But he still feels the harm from the remarks was more imagined than real. "I feel I took more of a whipping than I deserved." Still, Byrne says he answered all of the 200 to 250 calls, letters and faxes he received in the wake of the interview.

Despite the enormity of the task Byrne and the party faced, there did not seem to be the hurry that everyone would have liked in the fall of 1998. There was a sense "Christmas is coming, let's wait until January to get fund-raising in place." One party insider said the party talked to the people who would work on a publicity campaign, "our theme, our logo. All those discussions took place last fall. But Christmas is coming. Let's wait until January."

Byrne had done his best to see that the party had identified candidates in as many districts as possible. By September, twenty candidates were in place, and Byrne had good responses in many others, so much so that "he had almost every district covered off, with probably the exception of eight." Byrne and the others in the party knew however, that the crucial moment for potential candidates was still to come. How many would step forward once Brian Tobin said the election was on?

Parties in opposition face many challenges, either of which on its own is capable of putting a campaign off stride. Money was a challenge the Conservatives had coped with since the day in 1989 when Clyde Wells toppled the party from its seventeen year honeymoon with power. Heading into 1999, the Conservatives simply had no money.

That was a problem Loyola Hearn knew the party faced, even as he contemplated taking on the job as Ed Byrne's chief of staff. "We had none, I mean none," Hearn says, in relation to money. What had happened was this.

The party came out of the 1996 election owing $168,000. With just a handful of members, and with Brian Tobin's star continuing to rise, those who were elected knew raising funds would be as big a challenge as the election itself. Ed Byrne recalls trying to recruit people to ante up a few hundred dollars for a golf tournament. "Maybe five teams would show up, and we'd make $1200. Three years before, we'd have 20 teams and make $15,000." Loyola Sullivan, in his time as interim leader, whittled the debt down to about $70,000. Some of that was done with the election rebates Conservative candidates received from the Newfoundland Treasury, based on reaching a certain minimum percentage of votes in the election. [This section of the Elections Act benefits the Liberals in an even more substantial way, since they have elected more than 30 members in each of the last two elections, and since Liberal candidates have finished second or better in almost every district.]

Added to the $70,000 problem was a party debt Ed Byrne had discovered several years earlier while a member of the PC executive. Just after the 1985 election, Frank Ryan and John Ryan signed a $170,000 loan from the Royal Bank, on behalf of the PC party. Because of the setup of the party at the time, the PC party was separate from the party executive. The party was responsible for elections and it was under the direction of the leader. The executive was elected by party grassroots at a convention. When he was leader, Len Simms, saw it as an untenable situation and he brought the two groups together. Says Byrne, under the old system, "the provincial executive didn't know what was spent in an election."

By the early fall of 1999, that fourteen-year loan had been reduced to $120,0000, and the party was in discussions with the Royal Bank to "buy that down to about $30,000 or $40,000," meaning the Royal Bank would accept twenty-five cents for each dollar it was owed.

This then, was the situation that confronted Ed Byrne and the caucus when they met in the opposition party boardroom on the 5th floor of Confederation Building, one week before the election. One person who attended the meeting noted Byrne said "it's cash and carry on this one, folks," a clear message that with the till empty, the party could only spend money as it came in. Byrne outlined for the caucus and the members of the finance committee, his philosophy about spending, and the type of publicity campaign they could mount. "I said boys, I don't know what we're going to raise. If we raise $200,000, here's the type of media campaign we will run. If we raise $500,000, here's the type of media campaign we will run."

The challenge with having no money to run a campaign, is how to get started and prove to the public that the party actually has a plan. Prior to the election call, Byrne and his staff had worked out an advertising schedule and leaders' tour for the first 12 days of the campaign. The only way to get the plans from paper to reality though, was to have money. In order to do that, Byrne and four other party members went to their banks and each signed for a $15,000 line of credit. Those were the funds the party would use to get the campaign bus on the road, to open its headquarters, and put down deposits on everything from telephones to photocopiers. Those strict rules requiring deposits have been put in place by hesitant creditors, who had been stuck with Conservative party debt.

According to Loyola Hearn, "we had to wait a couple of days to get money enough to put our phones in. Almost everyone wanted a deposit. If you wanted to book ads — TV, radio, print ads — you had to have a certified cheque up-front."

Political leaders head their campaigns, they are expected to be morale boosters for the party, and to be models of positive thought for the three-week campaign. But the old style of running Conservative campaigns haunted Ed Byrne and people close to him heading into the 1999 vote. There was a long history in the Conservative party, and likely other parties, of hiding certain polling information from the leader. His own involvement with the party began in Brian Peckford's era, and so did Kim Puddister's association with the Conservatives.

Puddister is a close friend of Ed Byrne. She worked for John Crosbie when he was a federal cabinet minister, and she was Tom Rideout's executive assistant during the losing 1989 election campaign. Puddister believes people who have climbed into the leadership of a party have the smarts to not only take the bad news that can come from an opinion poll, they also have the experience to react to it in order to try and get a stalled campaign back in motion. Of the polling information that showed Conservative support slipping badly in the 1989 campaign she says, "I saw a Premier [Rideout] absolutely devastated because things were kept from him."

Ed Byrne was also aware of this kind of "political paternalism" on the part of the older men who generally ran political campaigns. He made it a point of reminding headquarters of this in his 11 o'clock nightly conference call from the road. "I said if anyone lies to me about anything, I will come in and kick somebody's arse."

Chapter 3

Three Candidates

Fall was turning into winter in Western Labrador. In his home on Vanier Avenue, Randy Collins was trying to finish painting a room. As the staff representative for the United Steelworkers of America in Labrador City, Collins was responsible for 23 bargaining groups, including negotiating contracts, working on arbitration cases, handling workers compensation complaints and employment insurance appeals. His position put him in close contact with political life in Western Labrador, and as he painted that afternoon, he kept thinking about a phone call he had received from St. John's the day before.

The call was from Chuck Furey, then Minister of Mines and Energy. Furey had hired Hatch and Associates to review a decision made earlier by the Iron Ore Company that it was more cost effective for the company to resurrect a pellet plant in Sept-Isles, Quebec, than it would be to expand their operation in Labrador City. On the surface, expansion in Labrador City would mean an additional 50 permanent jobs. More important though, it would signal a clear commitment to the area from IOC's new owners, North Limited. Furey now had the report, and asked Collins and the union president George Kean to come to St. John's for a meeting that Sunday at the Newfoundland Hotel. Collins and Kean were eager to have support for their position to have expansion take place in Labrador City, and were anxious to find out what the report concluded. Collins remembers, "they wanted to release the report to us. No one else in the province was aware of what the report contained at the time." The government, he says, promised "they would pay for everything. They would pay for our transportation, our hotels, meals, the whole thing. It wouldn't cost us a cent."

But the more Randy Collins thought about Furey's proposition, the more concern he felt. George Kean, it turned out, was having the same doubt about traveling to St. John's. He telephoned Collins and they both agreed "something didn't smell right." If the report backed expansion in Labrador City, the government would surely want to come in and release the report to the local people. Collins and Kean, with years of experience as union negotiators feared the worst, that the report Furey wanted to release to them supported IOC's decision to expand at Sept-Isles. It was an old political trick, they concluded. They would be expected to release the bad news when they arrived back in town. "We got together later in the day, tracked Furey down and said we won't be out", Collins recalls. ""We felt what would happen, is they would release the report to us, give us a copy, we'd come back to Labrador City. We'd be the ones who would have to answer all the questions."

Eventually, Furey came to town to release the report. As Collins and Kean feared, the Hatch report backed IOC's decision. The union and town and community leaders in Labrador City accused Hatch of not doing a thorough study, but the die was cast. The government would not try to intervene in IOC's decision. "The argument was not that they would lose money, it's that they wouldn't make as much," Collins said. "That really blew me away. I believed the test for the pellet plant in Labrador City should have been the standard used by the government for their stand on Voisey's Bay."

The strong feeling in Labrador City that the government didn't believe iron ore from their mine was worth fighting for, while the nickel ore from a potential mine at Voisey's Bay was the stuff that required not only strong political statement, but an almost shrill nationalistic outpouring, was too much for people to take. Overnight, an economic issue had become a political one, and Randy Collins began to think he might be the person to head the drive.

Randy Collins came to Labrador City in 1972. Prior to that, he had attended Memorial University in St. John's and worked part-time at the Bavarian Brewery on Leslie Street. IOC had a hiring office in St. John's, and with employment in western Labrador plentiful and with the lure of a permanent job, the 18-year old from Gambo signed up as a janitor. Two years later, Collins moved into a labour job at the mine. At the same time, his social conscience was aroused and he served on various union committees. IOC was a good place to work — the money was good and the company had its own training program. Collins took millwright training in 1974 . In two short years, he had gone from janitor to tradesman. By 1978, he joined the ruling body of the United Steelworkers in Labrador City, by getting elected to the union executive. Seven years later, he was union president. In 1991, he took on the job as staff representative for the United Steelworkers of America at Labrador City. And he even had a try at federal politics in the 1996 by-election, when Bill Rompkey retired from the Labrador seat after being appointed to the Senate. Collins placed a respectable second behind the current Member of Parliament, Liberal Lawrence O'Brien.

The long road through union politics had taught Collins a fundamental lesson. "Politics determines everything," Collins says. He recalled having negotiated "darn good increases for bus drivers and the government legislated them away. So politics does govern everything."

Collins concluded "the government sided with IOC" on the pellet plant issue, and it made no difference that the provincial representative for the district of Labrador West was on the government side. Perry Canning had first been elected in the Brian Tobin win in 1996. Prior to that, he had worked at IOC, and served with Collins on the union executive. And despite Collins' concern about the pellet plant issue, this personal side of his relationship with Perry Canning caused him to pause. "I was struggling with it," he says. "Perry Canning and I were, are, have been good friends for a long time. It wasn't like you were going to enter a race or an election between yourself and someone who you didn't really know, because Perry and I worked on a number of issues, prior to him being involved in politics."

The two men had cabins near each other on the Ashuanipi River near Labrador City. They visited each other there, and at home in Labrador City. Collins would have "no hesitation if I was driving along Hudson Drive of popping into Perry's house on the spur of the moment, or seeing him in the driveway and just stop by." Still, the political anger in Labrador City toward the government was too strong to ignore. Collins believes "you need people in government to represent the majority of people's views," and felt Canning was being loyal to the government's position instead of the people in his district.

Over Christmas, Collins ran into many friends and acquaintances who urged him to consider provincial politics when the election was called. "A lot of people and friends would come up to me and say 'you should do it'." He talked things over with his wife Gail, and pondered spending so much time away from home, "because I'd rather be in Labrador City any day of the week." In the end, the decision would be his.

Tom Hedderson comes from a family of 19. In early 1998, he let it be known in district party circles in Harbour Main-Whitbourne, that he was interested in going for the party's nomination for the next election. "I said maybe it's time for me to get involved," Hedderson recalls telling long-time party member Gerald Whalen of Colliers. Within days, Hedderson had "numerous calls" from people offering encouragement and help.

Hedderson was already entrenched in a career. Since leaving Memorial University with his teaching degree in 1975, he had taught in several communities in Conception Bay North. He enjoyed teaching, and later landed a job in administration as a principal. Newfoundland had been good to him, having been educated here, and for the past two decades, teaching in the province's school system. "It's time to give back," Hedderson concluded. Politics was in his blood, and he was determined to give it at least one try.

Most politicians recall their first political act, almost as if it were something equal to moral decay or some penultimate moment. For Tom Hedderson, it was the fractious dispute between Joey Smallwood and John Crosbie for the leadership of the Liberal Party in 1969. As a young educated Newfoundlander exposed to campus politics and the new age, Hedderson sided with Crosbie. And like many of his generation, this journey led him to the Progressive Conservatives. His political acts consisted of going door-to-door for Conservative candidates in the Harbour Main district, supporting candidates at nomination meets, and generally flying the Conservative flag.

In 1998, the provincial Conservative party was anxious to get as many candidates in place as possible. This strategy played into Hedderson's hands, and by mid-July he was the party's candidate in Harbour Main-Whitbourne. For the rest of the summer, Hedderson learned how to make contacts. "I ate more cold plates, went to more garden parties," he claims, as he attempted to let people know who he was and what he stood for. In a way, he was operating in political handcuffs. Yes, there was talk of an election, but it had not been called yet. Because of that, Hedderson could not raise money, but he did get pledges for donations.

Obtaining the nomination was helpful in another way. It allowed Hedderson to attend meetings of the Conservative caucus. That put him in direct contact with the leader, Ed Byrne, and it also allowed him to get to know party officials and the other members of caucus. And it gave him a head start on where the party was headed with respect to policy.

The real work though, was taking place in the district. Harbour Main-Whitbourne was represented by Liberal Don Whalen. It was already known he was going to be challenged by Wanda Dawe. Dawe and Hedderson got to know each other, by attending many of the same social and community functions. Hedderson's biggest challenge was exposing himself to as many people as possible. "I was known in some parts of the district," he says, "but in Whitbourne, for example, I wasn't known from Adam." So he took to turning up at events like the Whitbourne regatta. He called meetings at fire halls in the district, telling people why he was getting into politics and at the same time, looking for volunteers to help out on the campaign, when it came. "If the fire department was meeting on Thursday night, I asked, 'would you mind if I dropped in and introduced myself and answered a few questions?' It was a hard sell, they don't know you and they're wondering are you just one of those opportunists."

By September, with no election call, Hedderson was back as principal at Bishop O'Neill Collegiate in Brigus. But he was still carrying out his campaign, and spending his own money to do it. At Christmas, he sent a Christmas card to people in the district. It "was a big hit," he claims, especially since the Liberal MHA didn't send one.

Christmas would yield few clues about an election, but by the time Hedderson was back in school after the New Year, the countdown to an election would have begun quietly in the Premier's Office in St. John's.

Yvonne Jones was already a survivor of the political wars when talk surfaced in 1998 that Brian Tobin might call a snap vote. The native of Mary's Harbour, Labrador had nearly three years as an independent MHA under her belt, having served the district of Cartwright-L'anse au Clair. The road to her seat began in 1996 with a loss in the Liberal nomination to then-Liberal incumbent Danny Dumaresque. Jones decided to run as an independent in the election and won. Being elected as an independent has a certain allure to it. However, the fact remains Jones was sitting alone in the legislature, both literally and figuratively.

"The thing you don't have is the people around you, the teamwork approach to policy and legislation," she says of being an independent member. Summers in Cartwright-L'anse au Clair are busy times, given that most of the workforce is seasonal. Jones heard the election rumours, but "there was no certainty it would or would not come." Quietly, she set out to organize her election team and lay out a plan for the election, whenever it came. By fall, she had made up her mind that she would contest the Liberal nomination. This would be a rematch of the 1996 nomination against Danny Dumaresque.

In early January, Jones had to attend to family matters. Her maternal grandmother was seriously ill, and with all her brothers and sisters in other parts of the country, Jones turned away from politics for a few days to spend time with her mother. "It was a difficult time for my mother," she says. Days before the election, Jones' grandmother passed away.

Yvonne Jones had been in almost constant contact with Liberals in the days leading up to the election call. Ernie McLean, the Government Services and Lands minister was an especially keen supporter. On January 18th, all that remained to be done, was for Brian Tobin to announce the date. Yvonne Jones watched his televised news conference in her living room at Mary's Harbour. The race was on.

Jones' first nomination in 1996 had been a bitter fight. The Liberal Party wanted this one to be less so, and the candidates themselves felt under pressure to conform. In mid-January, certain that Brian Tobin would call the vote within days, Liberals mobilized in the district. A four-day nomination campaign was scheduled. Jones and Dumaresque worked their way up and down the coast, sharing an airplane owned by Tony Powell of Labrador Travel Air. "The plane picked me up, and dropped him off," says Jones. "That was pretty civilized."

Jones put everything into the nomination. "Whoever won the nomination would be the member at the end of the day," Jones thought. Her trips up and down the coast had convinced her "this was not going to be a PC or NDP seat."

Indeed, only for a few years in the early 1970's, has the southern Labrador Coast abandoned the Liberal Party. That was when Mike Martin of the upstart New Labrador Party won the district. This was a time of political awakening in Labrador, after decades of no political representation in the pre-Confederation days, and more than two decades of representation by the St. John's political gentry in the time since Confederation.

On the last evening of the nomination, Jones and Dumaresque shared Tony Powell's plane for the last time. They had been in each other's back yard all that day - Dumaresque in the northern coastal part of the district, and Jones in the Straits. At 5 o'clock, they passed each other on the tarmac at the airport in Blanc Sablon. "I was going out on the plane Danny was coming in on," says Jones. "We wished each other good luck."

Jones' road to politics had taken a roundabout route. She had left Mary's Harbour after finishing school, and attended journalism school. After brief stints with the Robinson-Blackmore community newspapers, and the-then *Evening Telegram*, she returned to Labrador to work with Memorial University's Institute of Northern Studies in Happy Valley-Goose Bay. It was there that she met her future husband Jim, also a native of Mary's Harbour. After getting married, they moved back to Mary's Harbour. Yvonne Jones took a job as an employment officer with the federal government, and worked in a number of community and regional economic and social development agencies. In 1992, she became mayor of Mary's Harbour. By the time of the 1996 election, Jones "didn't feel challenged enough" and "felt frustrated dealing with governments." That was when she took the move toward provincial politics.

Although Mike Martin had made the same trek from social and economic development into provincial politics 25 years before, Jones was of a new generation on the coast who felt "disincluded" in the political life of the province. "The Straits was always very comfortable with politics," she says, of the area of the district connected by 60 kilometres of paved road from L'anse au Clair to Red Bay. "They were very active participants in elections." In the isolated coastal part of the district, politics was of interest to the few. "You had one or two people in every community who took care of things for you." When Jones ran in 1996, "this was all new on the coast. You had to motivate people to get them out [campaigning]"

A large group had gathered at the airport in Mary's Harbour to welcome Yvonne Jones home to await the nomination results. As the plane taxied in, they cheered her arrival. Jones sat with her family and friends and waited for the returns. Some of the polls were close, but she took the nomination by a couple of hundred votes.

The nomination was over, Yvonne Jones was the Liberal candidate, the party she wanted to represent in 1996.

Chapter 4

Lead-Up

Brian Tobin looked out his eighth floor office window at the parking lot where ministers, backbenchers and the opposition members park their cars. He was pleased. It was just after the New Year holiday, and hardly anyone was stirring. He had pretty much made up his mind on an election call over the Christmas holiday. The challenge now was to gear up, get a strategy in place, and then let his cabinet in on the secret. He told senior staff of his plans, what he needed of them in preparing an agenda for the couple of weeks prior to an election, and pledged them to stay quiet. "I started assigning responsibilities very quietly," he says. "It [the news of an election] wasn't out in the rank and file, it wasn't a final decision." But within three days of being back at work, the decision was final. The circle of those in the know began to widen.

Cabinet ministers were among the first to sense the new urgency in the Premier's Office. One-by-one they were called in by Tobin in the first ten days of January to review the goings-on in their departments. Tobin wanted to know the various projects and plans his ministers had on the drawing board. More important, what was the agenda they planned to bring forward in the next few weeks and months? "I knew right off the bat, I could see he was contemplating an election," said one minister. Not only did the Premier meet with ministers individually, he met with the various committees of cabinet. While it is individual ministers and departments that develop plans, it is in the various committees that priorities are set and action is planned.

Tobin's sense of urgency could have been the result of any number of factors, but only one, a potential nurses' strike, seemed to be of any substance. Some insiders claim Tobin began to contemplate the effect of a nurses' strike just before Christmas. If he wanted to avoid a fall 1999 election, there were just two windows of opportunity in the winter-spring period. One such window was the time between mid-January and the beginning to the two-week long Canada Winter Games at Corner Brook. The second "safe" period was just after the Games, and before a potential nurses' strike in early April. As much as Tobin had been seized with the "timing" issue the previous summer, when he worried the public might rebel against an early election and vote against the government, he was now faced with a different kind of timing problem. He could either get the election over before the Games and while the Liberals were still high in the polls, or wait, and suffer the possible consequences of a nurses' strike and a riled-up public that would have much to say about the state of the healthcare system.

As Tobin called his cabinet ministers in for briefings on their plans, he already had a plan in place to begin selling the government's agenda. It would be done in a way that was similar to how he spread announcements in the summer. Said one minister, "Brian is very clever at electioneering." He intended to get his announcements out of the way prior to the election call "rather than call an election and make all of these promises". And so it was that economic development spending under the post-TAGS program was announced, funding for tourism projects, and various other plans. "If you don't have press conferences and then got out and hand out the cheque, people think you're not doing anything," commented one Liberal MHA.

After these meetings, the Liberals played the announcements game like a finely tuned violin, both in the days leading up to the election call, and in certain strategic cases, during the campaign. There were at least 50 press releases issued from government departments through January and early February. The first releases generally focused on good news, ministers noting that certain things had been done or had happened, and that this was cause for rejoicing. This began in the week after the New Year's holiday. The second stage was more direct — announcements of millions of dollars to fund specific projects and programs.

Tobin himself suggests the announcements would have come anyway. "We had been dealing with hospital funding for some time, we had held discussions with the university. What people may have found a little unusual is that we announced them before the election. We dealt with those issues because they had gone through the cabinet system." Tobin argues the decision to get all the announcements out before the election was part of a strategy to allow people to focus on what he felt were the "larger issues," such as Voisey's Bay and Churchill Falls. It would become clear however, that the timing and frequency of the announcements was an effort to build momentum heading into the campaign, and to put the government's "record" up against the promises from the opposing parties. He does concede "we accelerated them [the announcements] in the period of time prior to the election, no question."

The "feel-good news" began dripping out on January 5th, when Judy Foote told the public that students in Rigolet were now attending a new school. It was all proof that education reform was paying dividends, she claimed. Foote noted that $125 million in school construction and renovation funds had now been promised, evidence that "government is committed to schools that are maintained at the highest possible standard." A day later, Foote was back with another statement. Contrary to comments by the teachers association, she argued, education reform was indeed working. And so it went all that week after the Christmas/New Year break, statements reacting to calls for gas price regulation; the minister of Municipal and Provincial Affairs promising 1999 would bring a new approach to municipal relations. In that statement, Lloyd Matthews foreshadowed announcements that would come the week after, to assist in "meeting challenges facing municipalities in the province." Paul Dicks, the Finance Minister, reported being pleased a controversy had been resolved about the appointment of Nova Scotian Peter Kelly as general manager of the Marble Mountain ski resort. Kelly had been pilloried both by some west coast residents who believed a Newfoundlander could have been found for the job, and by the press. Dicks said Kelly would not get the job. The same day as Dicks' statement, Chuck Furey was outlining a five-city Soiree marketing tour, aimed at the 1999 tourism season. That might have been intended as a clever diversion for the press and opposition. The statement said he and the Premier would travel to five cities in late January and early February. But the dates — practically all of them —conflicted what would eventually be the election period.

Other announcements in this first phase, intended to create a positive image of the government, flew out of Confederation Building at the rate of several each day. Works, Services and Transportation said the government would borrow to finance construction of the Harbour Breton health care building rather than finance it under a fund made up of low-interest loans from immigrant investors; the Education department approved financing for nine school groups from rural areas to travel to and experience life in urban regions; Human Resources and Employment and the Department of Finance reported the province had its strongest year of economic and employment growth so far in the 1990's; there was a release commending federal fisheries for its five-year trout management plan; and the Marble Mountain managers issued a release proclaiming it was not political influence "nor comments by the opposition, nor the fact that Mr. Kelly is from Nova Scotia," that resulted in their decision to can Peter Kelly.

The next stage of announcements, timed for the week of January 11, were the real meat of the government's pre-election politicking. On the Tuesday before the election call, $1.5 million was announced as a contribution toward the clean-up of St. John's Harbour. The next day, Brian Tobin unveiled a tax credit program to help finance a Newfoundland movie industry, "a new opportunity for economic and employment growth." The same day, the government announced a pre-emptive strike to critics concerned about the state of healthcare. $20 million dollars would be spent, most of it to go toward covering the deficit built up by hospital boards in the province, the remainder toward purchase of some new equipment. Tobin summoned senior hospital administrators from across the province to Confederation Building to receive the good news and to react to this new commitment.

The Liberals had been given a bloody nose by the City of St.

John's in the fall of 1998, largely because Mayor Andy Wells and some councillors felt the province wasn't paying enough to the city as compensation for water, sewer, fire protection, and other services provided by the city. The harbour clean-up funding was part of a response by the government, and so was an announcement by Municipal Affairs Minister, and St. John's North MHA Lloyd Matthews on January 13. The province had completed a review on the water tax issue he said, and concluded "fair payment of the water tax" would be $700,000 in addition to the $174,000 already being paid to the city. This was an increase of about 400 percent! Worried about the overall state of relations with the capital city, Matthews added "the provincial government is interested in establishing a cooperative working relationship with the city council in an effort to benefit all residents of St. John's."

Governments know elections can be lightning rods for any number of public issues, both large provincial ones and smaller, but important, local issues. Healthcare and the government's relationship with the City of St. John's were very large issues, and if not properly addressed, they both had the capacity to imperil incumbents in a large number of seats. Healthcare affected all residents of the province, while St. John's issues could directly affect nine seats. Education concerns, both in the regular school system and the post-secondary system, also loomed as potential trouble-makers. Post-secondary education, especially in the public colleges and the university, had endured a decade of steady and unpopular hikes in tuition rates. If those issues were not tackled, a winter election would put the government face-to-face with students who were still in school in the major centres. Students know how to create a fuss and public profile for an issue, and worse still for politicians who practice problem avoidance, they have the time to commit to demonstration and protest.

Brian Tobin and his education minister Judy Foote knew of student concerns. They had known in the fall that some form of tuition assistance would be a partial solution. On January 14th, four days before the election call, Tobin and Foote promised $11.9 million in extra funding to the College of the North Atlantic, the organization that operates the group of community and regional public colleges, and to Memorial University. Tobin said this was done "in the hopes that it will allow both the university and the college to freeze their tuition levels for the next two years." Without such a promise, Tobin would likely have had groups of students on his tail during the campaign. Memorial President Art May glowed, "no tuition increase is the best birthday present that government could give to Memorial University students on the 50th anniversary as a degree-granting institution." And Vince Withers, who had been touted as a potential candidate for Liberals and Conservatives, said in his capacity as chairman of the board of College of the North Atlantic, "government has recognized the need to respond constructively to the pressing needs of students and the college."

In the New Democratic camp, leader Jack Harris was by now convinced Tobin was in election mode. His family's January vacation plans were put on hold, and Harris began contacting the party executive. Even with the feverish state of Tobin's activity in those early days of January, Harris had to convince some that "this is drop-everything time." The New Democrats though, were not ready for a winter election. "We didn't have an election planning team in place," says Harris. "There was a fair amount of scrambling going on."

Harris's immediate challenge was to find enough candidates to field a team. "I started phoning around," he says, telling prospective candidates, "this could happen in a few days." It was all too much of a distraction for a leader who would be expected to headline the NDP campaign, to have to map out details for the campaign. But that's just what Harris was involved with in the weekend before the election call. "As party leader, I shouldn't have to be worried [about the details]," he says. He and party members met and worked out an itinerary for the first couple of days of the campaign.

Their plan was to run as many candidates as the NDP could find, but the strategy was to focus on a few seats where the party would poll well. "We thought it was possible to win 3, 4, or 5 seats," says Harris. Their focus would be St. John's, where the vote split could favour NDP candidates. Two other regions that showed promise were

Western Labrador, where the Steelworkers in Labrador City and Wabush could be counted on to promote the party, especially with the pellet plant issue involving the Iron Ore Company of Canada mine at Labrador City, and Burin-Placentia West, which included Marystown and the hundreds of union members there. The party also felt there might be some benefit in the provincial seats that made up the federal riding of Bonavista-Trinity-Conception. Former labour leader Fraser March had polled well there in the 1997 federal election, actually winning the vote in some of the districts. "We had a sense of the possibilities," says Harris, but unfortunately for the party, "organizationally we were deficient."

And Harris had to think about his own seat, Signal Hill-Quidi Vidi. Harris had represented the former district of St. John's East, but under redistribution prior to the 1996 election, part of the district was removed, and the core of his constituency was renamed. Harris felt redistribution had planted a solid Liberal area in his district, and he suspected "they [the Liberals] wanted somebody to run against me and to keep me in the district." For the leader of a party with just one seat, such concerns "can be distracting" admits Harris.

For the Liberals, the pieces were falling into place. Over the two days heading into the weekend before the election call, a few more announcements were made, including a decision to reinstate municipal grants the government had previously intended to take away. The Federation of Municipalities called the announcement "positive." This was followed by a statement from Paul Dicks that Newfoundland's finances were in good shape, and that while the deficit was up from what the government had projected in its three-year plan, there was reason for confidence. "We will not reach into the pockets of Newfoundlanders and Labradorians for more money," Dicks promised.

Announcements provide exposure for the government and for the politicians involved. Everyone inside the Liberal party knew Labrador West Liberal Perry Canning was facing a strong challenge over the plan by the Iron Ore Company to reopen its Sept-Isles, Quebec pellet plant, rather than expand its operation at Labrador

City. To counter some of this feeling, and to promote Canning's profile, decisions were made to include him in some of the announcements. Tobin included Canning at the head table during several announcements on January 15th at the Newfoundland Hotel. Canning announced on behalf of Kevin Aylward, the opening of the Seal Lake Caribou Zone in Labrador. Canning also had his name attached to a press release from Mines and Energy Minister Roger Grimes that IOC had agreed to a "comfort letter" for workers at their Labrador City mine. While the wording of the letter would be worked out in negotiations with the union, IOC had promised to keep the workforce at its current levels in the event of a downturn in the economy. Said Canning, "any fear of this future negative outcome [job losses], has now been removed."

Late in the afternoon of the Friday before the election, the Justice Department moved to quell fears in an area bordering the School for the Deaf in St. John's, that it had abandoned plans to place the new youth remand centre adjacent to the school.

Despite all this public activity, and the apparent obvious purpose for it, cabinet ministers were under orders to let no one know of the plans that were in the works. But no ship is waterproof, and their masters know political ships will spring leaks no matter how tough the orders.

Ed Byrne and the rest of the Conservative MHA's have their offices on the fifth floor of Confederation Building. Liberals might not tell the Conservatives their plans, but by early January, "we started getting weird rumours," according to one source. The conflicting rumours either had an election in January just prior to the Winter Games, or at some time later in the spring. The Conservatives, who had put much of their heavy pre-election work off until early in the new year, now went at the job aggressively.

"We started working around the clock," according to Kim Pudister. The party had its public relations advisors in, as well as the all-important fund-raising team. Within a day, the public relations team had some samples for Ed Byrne and his team to consider. The fund-raising team would find the going a little more challenging. But the biggest challenge was one that was proving to be a nightmare in the making — many of the potential candidates Ed Byrne had lined up the previous fall, were now withdrawing.

On the Liberal side, certain key ministers began letting the word drop in conversations that an election was "imminent." Tobin himself was dispatching his chief of staff Gerry Glavine and his executive assistant Tony Grace to ask various people to take on particular roles in the campaign. The week before the election call, the final arrangements were made. Staff at party headquarters made plans to lease cell phones, to check on the availability of rental cars and helicopters. One person in the tour office was given exclusive responsibility for monitoring weather conditions. This was especially important given that this was a winter election, and travel by air to remote areas of the south coast, northern peninsula and Labrador could be thrown off if conditions deteriorated. And that meant using sources in addition to the weather office to get a full picture in advance of announcing Tobin's visit to any region. Said one person at central office, "you watch the weather. You check with local organizers on weather. A coastal community could be fogged in and Gander weather office may not know."

Seasoned Liberals involved with the campaign detected a changed and more relaxed Brian Tobin from his first provincial campaign in 1996. In 1996, "he was totally dependent on people he hadn't worked with before. I think he was more concerned in that campaign than in this one." The source said Tobin was "demanding but not so intensely demanding" as he was in 1996, and that might have been because "he had confidence in those around him. When he was up in the air, [he knew] there would be a car or bus there when he landed."

Election Diary

Friday, January 15, 1999

The speculation about an election began this week, and it continues, unabated. And with good reason. Tobin is at the Delta Hotel in downtown St. John's with Newfoundland Transshipment to announce a $65-million expansion to their terminal at Whiffen Head, Placentia Bay. This will create over 100 jobs for an 18 month period. Tobin jokingly tells President Harvey Mott "this makes my announcements pale by comparison."

Not quite. At 2:30 that afternoon at the Newfoundland Hotel, Tobin, Fred Mifflin, Labrador MHA Perry Canning and MP Lawrence O'Brien announce $86.85-million worth of economic development funding, as well as funds for the coming Soiree celebrations, and funding for enhancing snowmobile trails in Labrador.

Tobin is again asked about an election. He answers coyly. I ask him the same question at a press briefing after the news conference. He replies that sometime in the next few days he will end the election speculation at a news conference. At least the time frame is being narrowed.

Conspicuous by his presence in the room is Wayne Guzzwell. A former CBC television producer, Guzzwell has been in charge of producing the Cabot landing at Bonavista, the Canada Winter Games (1 year away) bash at Corner Brook, and the 1998 New Years Eve bash at the St. John's waterfront. He's likely in charge of producing or coordinating election spots for Tobin.

He's had a television crew from Bristol Communications shooting the news conference on extra funding for healthcare and the Whiffen Head announcement.

I have other things on my mind. My son has a hockey tournament tomorrow and Sunday. I'm coaching. I plan to put the election on the back burner for a couple of days.

Election Diary

Saturday, January 16, 1999

I figure the guessing about an election is nearly finished.

This evening, on the way to town with my son to pick up a toy, I saw the evidence that an election call was imminent. A dozen cars were parked outside the Liberal Party offices on Peet Street. The Party was gearing up for the call.

Election Diary

Monday, January 18, 1999

Newsrooms are rumour hatcheries, and today is no different. Everyone has a theory on when and why Tobin will make the election at a particular time. I've been involved in ten elections (6 provincial and 4 federal) and guessing is something I avoid. There's a rather simple explanation — reporters are usually wrong, and it keeps them from pursuing other stories.

I spent the morning on the phone. First to Heidi Bonnell in the Premier's Office to arrange a four minute interview with Tobin after the election announcement. She thought that would be okay and promised to get back to me. That never happened.

I talked to an MHA and a cabinet minister. The cabinet minister told me he was now convinced the election call would be today. He was not so sure on Friday. It's all in the Premier's hands. It drove home for me how vulnerable these politicians must feel — their careers are in the hands of one person. Even if they disagree with a decision that could put them out of a job — and a pension — they have to stand there with the group at the announcement and look happy, very happy.

The radio morning news had the election call coming at four o'clock this afternoon. That may have been the case at one point. But the sands change quickly in politics. By late morning, reporters were speculating about two o'clock. Then three o'clock. A Liberal MHA told me the word to the caucus was to be around Confederation Building by three o'clock.

As the afternoon went on, it was clear Here & Now's plans for tonight's coverage would have to change. We had planned to have stories on the announcement, the Conservatives' and New Democrats' day, then interviews and reaction to the election call from the party leaders. We would round it all out with a three-person panel — Conservative Janice Wells from Corner Brook, New Democrat Roy Locke from Gander and Liberal Jim Walsh from St. John's. So much for plans.

By three-thirty, it was time to make firm plans. The plant manager and technical director were called into a meeting with the producers and myself. Could we do the show live from Confederation Building, as we now had to deal with the possibility of an election call at six-thirty, the start time for our show? We could, but the risk of a technical foul-up was great. The decision was made to have me anchor the show out of the studio. Then the word came Tobin was holding the news conference at six-thirty. It might not have been our preference, but at least we now could make some firm plans.

Rick Seaward would be in the Liberal caucus room and we would go to him at the top of our show.

Jay Callanan would be in the Conservative room and do the same.

Jack Harris was lined up to come in for a live interview.

We finally had the pieces together.

Our show would look different than it did most nights, but we'd have the top story covered. The challenge now was to keep Tobin to some reasonable period of time. After all, this was an election announcement on the highest-rated news show in Newfoundland and Labrador. I was concerned we not let him have any more than eight minutes. As it was, we stayed with him for 13 minutes. I gritted my teeth watching some of it, as I believed we had given him too much time. I thought we should have pulled out after about 10 minutes and all we would have missed was the boosterism.

I felt a little better after we joined Ed Byrne's presentation. We also let his speech run to the end. The balance we all wanted to be there, was present, more or less. Byrne though, had five minutes less than Tobin.

I also couldn't help but notice, despite the small crowd at Byrne's announcement, how energetic he appeared. He also hit the issues forcefully. I don't believe in counting anyone out in a political race. Ed Byrne proved tonight that he belongs in the race. 21 days though, is a long time to keep it all together.

Jack Harris came into the studio while Byrne was on-air. He watched and waited while we went through a few election-related stories, the weather pre-

view, and several commercials. It wasn't lost on Harris, that our report about the kickoff to his campaign gave about 30 seconds to Pete Soucy, a man fighting for the Liberal nomination in Harris's district. He passed it off in a light way, but Harris did not appear to be amused.

Here & Now went smoothly, proof that even with major cutbacks in recent years, our small crew of people can do the job when it gets challenging.

Chapter 5

The Call

The coffee was on early in the Premier's Office. Brian Tobin had decided this was the day to call the election. All the plans had been made, the policy document completed, the television and print ads were in place, the campaign bus was ready, and the campaign office was ready to swing into action. All that was left to do now was to officially tell cabinet and the caucus that Tobin would visit the Lieutenant Governor late in the afternoon to ask for dissolution of the legislature. The latest polling information showed the government holding strong. Privately, Tobin and other Liberals were thinking of 40 seats, if things went right.

It was a relatively short cabinet meeting. After telling his ministers he was ready to spring them into an election, Tobin went around the table one more time to hear what people had to say. Unlike the situation in the near-election in late summer, this time, there were no dissenters. One minister remembers, "he had it all organized, the advertising, all the machinery was lined up, the campaign strategy was defined, the mandate to be sought was defined." Tobin had commenced some of this preparatory work in the fall "so it was really a matter of kicking it into gear." The ministers were in a good mood. Most had been asked their view of things well before this day, and they all felt plugged into the big decision. Said one Liberal, "he involves the people around him, he would have been seeking advice from cabinet." Still, despite their concurrence with Tobin's plan, some found the meeting "nerve-wracking." "You do not know until you go to the meeting that day, that he's calling an election. Until this thing is called, it is not a reality." Tobin had one final bit of advice for his ministers — "don't give any indication [to the press or anyone else]...it's business as normal." Even with people expecting the election call that day, ministers were told it was wise to keep the opposition off-guard for as long as possible.

The elected Liberals who are not part of the cabinet had to be told as well, so a meeting of the full caucus was arranged for the afternoon. "We've been told to expect a meeting anytime after three," said one backbencher, anxiously anticipating the election call. The Liberal caucus room is adjacent to the legislature. A large rectangular-shaped dark wooden table sits in the middle of the room, surrounded by swivelling brown leather chairs. The table is shaped so that every member can see any other member, and it was from here that Brian Tobin planned to launch his campaign later in the evening.

As Liberals filed into the room for caucus, most knew this was the moment that had been talked about and speculated on since last summer. There was a poignancy that many found difficult to reconcile with the nervous energy they all felt, since they were about to voluntarily put their jobs on the line, eighteen months ahead of when they would normally go to the polls. "You're looking around that room," said one Liberal, "you know this whole group, you have a team here, it's going to change. Everyone is looking at each other in the same way, saying 'who's going to be back?'". John Efford has had many large majorities since he was first elected in 1985. Still, he found himself looking around the room and wondering. "You look around the table, if there's 35 or 37 members, you wonder am I going to be here? Is Chuck [Furey] going to be here? Is Kevin [Aylward] going to be here?" Kevin Aylward, as it turned out, was having his own good look at a caucus whose makeup was bound to change. "It's very human, you're walking the plank and you wonder who's going to come back."

Brian Tobin went over the same speech as he did in cabinet. But caucus is the entire elected group of Liberals, so this was also a political speech. He wanted his members to be motivated by this speech, so Tobin heaved on the rhetoric. He was the one to negotiate tough with INCO on Voisey's Bay, and a Liberal government would have the resolve to do it right. It was he who had negotiated an agreement-in-principle with Quebec on Churchill Falls hydro, and a Liberal government comprised of a new generation would correct the injury that Newfoundland had suffered with the old Churchill Falls deal. But all the rhetoric could not overcome the empathy Tobin and others in the room had for one of their group, Labrador West MHA Perry Canning.

The government's decision to concur with IOC on the pellet plant issue had cast Canning adrift. The first-term MHA would have to go back to his district and do the best he could. He was largely on his own, and it seemed, everyone knew it. One member recalls Tobin singling Canning out for "special recognition" during the caucus, "everybody knew Perry was going to be in tough. The Premier indicated, 'Perry, we're going to do everything we can here to make sure you come through this.'" But Perry Canning was a sacrificial lamb in a system where the Premier can call the election when he wants. One member said "if Perry was probably giving advice to the Premier, he might have hoped for the election to be later, and wait for this issue [the pellet plant] to fade a bit."

Canning was not the only member who knew things would be tough. Bill Ramsey in Lapoile would be in for a severe test for the Liberal nomination. Kevin Aylward, who, as a cabinet minister, had regional responsibility for Lapoile, recalls "Bill knew he was in trouble. I did too." John Efford also sensed that his good friend Melvin Penney from Lewisporte would have a tough time. Penney had a residence in St. John's, something Efford says can hurt a member. "If there's any particular issue that comes up, they feel that you left them out. That you're not there." Efford also knew it would be a big challenge for the Liberals to retain Harbour Main-Whitbourne. Wanda Dawe defeated the incumbent Liberal MHA Don Whalen in the nomination. But being from Bay Roberts, which was outside the district would likely hurt. Efford says for Dawe to have won "would have been a hell of a victory, because she was looked at as a parachute candidate."

Even as caucus met, the government publicity machine was at work. At 3:05 on January 18, a press release was sent to newsrooms across the province, and no doubt, to town and community councils, that tenders were being called for 21 road projects. The projects, valued at $43.4 million, would have been called anyway at some time during the late winter. But there was no use waiting, not with an election call about to be made. The projects would see work done in more than a dozen districts, and considering that many of the roads connected with other districts, such an announcement could do no harm.

The Liberals attempted to cover all the bases. In an effort to preempt unsuccessful Liberal candidates at nomination meetings from running as independents or as candidates for other parties, each candidate was required to sign an affidavit, called Affirmation of Principles. This issue had bugged the Liberals in a couple of elections under Clyde Wells in Lapoile and St. George's in 1993, and in the 1996 election in Cartwright-L'Anse au Clair. The affidavit read, "I, the undersigned...undertake to support the candidacy of whosoever shall be the Liberal candidate and not seek election as an independent candidate or as a candidate for another political party." While party spokesman Fred Rowe didn't believe there was "any legal basis" that would prevent an unsuccessful candidate from doing what the affidavit appeared to preclude, he allowed "if signed, it would be pretty dishonourable to run against the Affirmation of Principles."

While the Liberals contemplated the political implications of a situation they were on the verge of creating because of the election call, the Conservatives were waiting to find out the details. "We were going crazy" is how one party worker remembers the day of the election call. "Our biggest concern was that he [Tobin] was going to shut us out in terms of media and he tried his best." Conservatives feared Tobin would call the election late in the day, when media, especially television and radio, are concerned with meeting deadlines.

Ed Byrne called a meeting of his election team for one o'clock, still not sure when exactly Tobin would call the election. Everything was as ready as it could be at this late hour. They would have to scramble to find candidates for about half the districts within the first week after the election call. The Blue Book, containing the campaign platform, was ready. There was concern though, that a couple of the policy statements were rushed into the platform. Loyola Hearn remembers questions about the makeup of regional healthcare boards. The platform implied the boards should be done away with, and the hired officials at particular hospitals should report directly to St. John's. The second issue that led to some concern was the language surrounding assistance for business. The platform suggested a Conservative government would do away with all support to business, when according to Hearn, "what we were trying to say was 'the time for giveaways is over', there are ways of helping business without handing out money."

The Conservatives felt it was not the policy document itself that was deficient, but the fact they needed "to have some more input. We had party input, but probably not as much as we would have liked with the grassroots," said one party member. "We would have liked to have taken the document and feed it out to people, to business people," for instance.

By mid-afternoon, with cabinet and caucus having been briefed, Tobin and the Liberals knew they could not hide the election call any longer. The government information service sent a notice to newsrooms that the Premier would hold a news conference at 6:30 in the Liberal caucus room at Confederation Building. It was timed to get the maximum television exposure for the Liberals. — the announcement would come at the start of CBC's *Here & Now*, and in the middle of NTV's newscast. Not only that, the 6:30 start would ensure coverage on CBC Newsworld's *Politics* with Don Newman, a must watch for politicians and their aides in Ottawa. Brian Tobin liked nothing more than to steal the national media spotlight and to set tongues wagging in Ottawa about his motive for calling a vote less than three years into his mandate.

While Liberals gathered around their leader at the news conference in St. John's, the Conservatives made a plan of their own to have Ed Byrne appear live on *Here & Now* with his own announcement. Although just down the hall from the Liberals, it was out of range of NTV's transmission. CBC had made the decision to go live with both announcements once it had become known Tobin planned to make the election call at the start of *Here & Now*. The Conservatives' fear earlier in the day of being frozen out, had now dissipated. Says Byrne's executive assistant Kim Puddister, "He [Tobin] didn't want us getting any media, we surprised him because we had a crowd, we had our book and we rushed Ed Byrne in with his caucus."

Still, Tobin had another trick to try. All the media covering his campaign, some of whom were planning to cover Byrne's event, were told Tobin was leaving for Corner Brook immediately after his announcement. In other words, there would be no time for them to see Ed Byrne's event and hear what he had to say. Kim Puddister remembers the Canadian Press reporter running down the hallway from Tobin's news conference saying "I really have to go. Do you have a release and your policy book?"

Jack Harris didn't wait for Brian Tobin's event. Along with a couple of candidates, he appeared at a new conference in the late afternoon announcing the party's platform, with its emphasis on social policy, especially healthcare and education. He viewed Brian Tobin's live news conference as "too clever by half," convinced that "that kind of apparent manipulation of media and events bred a certain resentment [in the public]." And as Brian Tobin announced the election at 6:30, Harris sat in Ray Guy's faux leather chair in the *Here & Now* studio and waited to do a live interview. Harris curtly dismisses Brian Tobin's claim the issue was who would lead the negotiations on Voisey's Bay and Churchill Falls. Says Harris, "this was just Tobin taking advantage of the fact the polls were in his favour now and perhaps wouldn't be in the future."

As Newfoundland and Labrador watched the news unfold that evening, candidates and potential candidates knew this was the minute they had planned for. In Harbour Main-Whitbourne, Tom Hedderson, who had been in place for more than six months, developed a case of the jitters. "I was frightened to death," he recalls. "What if someone says to me on page 15 of your Blue Book (the Conservative policy platform), your party says they are going to do this. What if I say the wrong thing? What if they phone Ed Byrne and say Tom Hedderson doesn't know what's on page 15 of the Blue Book? I was scrambling and thought about every scenario of every question."

In Mary's Harbour on the southern Labrador coast, Yvonne Jones had the challenge of running a campaign, despite a widelyheld view that Liberal votes would outnumber support for the Conservatives by six or seven to one. Some constituents even suggested to her that there was no need to campaign. But Jones is a veteran of two nomination fights and one district campaign prior to the 1999 election, and she knew nothing is certain in an election. She worried people might get complacent, now that the highly-charged nomination battle was over. "I was concerned people would not vote on election day." The Conservatives had very shallow roots in the district and the New Democrats had virtually none. Jones decided the election campaign would take the form of a tour, with as many door-to-door visits as possible. She and her husband Jim would hit the road.

Election Diary

Monday, January 18, 1999
Part II

I've heard a bit of gossip from the West Coast.

Eddie Joyce, who gave up his seat for Clyde Wells in 1989, and then decided to not run in 1996 so that Brian Tobin could have a west coast constituency, wants back into politics.

He's been ten years working for Wells and Tobin. I'm told he's been badgering Tobin and others that it's time he got the chance to run for a seat. That's why Tobin has decided to run in The Straits-White Bay.

Gerald Smith, the Liberal for Port au Port, has been passed over a couple of times for cabinet. On one occasion, in the lead-up to the Term 17 campaign on education reform, he turned down Clyde Wells' invitation because he could not support removing the churches from the school system. I'm told he's disappointed Tobin hasn't put him in cabinet and on a couple of occasions, he's asked Liberals "what's the point" of staying in politics if he's to remain on the backbenches.

Election Diary

Tuesday, January 19

The Brian Tobin tour is in Corner Brook and on the Northern Peninsula today. He's getting his nomination settled in The Straits — White Bay, the district that was held by Chris Decker.

Ed Byrne is in St. John's accompanying Paul Brown around St. John's Centre, the district held by Health and Community Services Minister Joan Marie Aylward. Brown is an interesting story. He lost by a couple of hundred votes to Aylward in 1996 and has been a presence in the district since, helping people with problems navigate their way through the provincial bureaucracy. Brown had his office set up two months before the election, with a computerized database of all the electors. If trying and organization counts, he should be close on election night. But he's facing a cabinet minister.

Jack Harris is still in St. John's and he's trying to get candidates in place. He told me in an interview last night he doesn't think it's necessary to have a candidate in each district in order to be seen as credible.

Today, I was on my own search for an election story. It took me to the Human Resources offices in downtown St. John's. People also know it as the unemployment office. I wanted to get a couple of people's stories about their efforts to find jobs.

Fred was anxious to talk. He's a short order cook, is married, has a house in Mount Pearl and he and his wife have a baby on the way. He works two jobs part-time, one in an Avalon Mall fast food restaurant, the other in a bakery. He was carrying a sportsbag. Fred told me he always carries a change of clothing. He finishes his shift at the Mall, changes into his bakery clothes, then heads off to the second job. Other days, like today, he has dress clothes in there. He's on the hunt for a second job, because he's getting a lay-off from his job at the Mall on Saturday. Fred isn't a quitter. If he doesn't find any jobs he's qualified for, he changes into the dress clothes and goes knocking on doors. He tells me he will find something.

Fred knows part of the way out of his predicament with minimum wage, part-time jobs is to go back to school for more training. The only problem is there are large waiting lists for the programs and he's near the end of the line. He'll just keep on knocking on doors.

Trina has just finished a four-year Arts program at Memorial. She helped put herself through university with part-time, minimum wage jobs. Now she has a large student loan, and low-paying jobs don't return enough to make her loan payments. Trina makes the trip in from Torbay every morning with her sister, who has a job in town. She had given herself a month to find employment, but now realizes it may be more reasonable to wait longer in order to get answers back from the employers she's written. After a couple of months, she may have to consider other options. "Which options?" I ask. "Going away, to Ontario." Trina, like most of Newfoundland and Labrador, has relatives there. She's on the verge of becoming another out-migration statistic. And she's young — part of a group that actually lost ground in the employment wars in Newfoundland in 1998.

A few hours later, I'm in a hot studio chatting with Liberal MHA Jim Walsh, Conservative hopeful Janice Wells and New Democrat Roy Locke. This is the interview that was sidelined by the election call yesterday. The talk doesn't centre around Fred's and Trina's concerns, it's why the election was called this early, how the government seems to be able to find money for programs when it's facing the electorate, and what Brian Tobin's real motives are when he calls an election two years early. Prior to the interview, the banter between Wells and Walsh is respectful, barely. Wells thinks an election now is unnecessary, and that Tobin is doing it so he can be free to chase after the Prime Minister's job when Jean Chretien leaves. Walsh shoots back about the Conservatives being so desperate for candidates, they're attempting to bring former leaders Tom Rideout and Lynn Verge back. Roy Locke doesn't get involved in the discussion.

Election Diary

Wednesday, January 20, 1999

This is the second straight day Ed Byrne has signed a contract on a large posterboard. This one is on education, and it pledges the Conservatives to implement their policies if they are elected. It's catching people's attention, but the question remains — will it be seen as a ploy to get attention rather than the serious attention he wants to focus on education?

A blow to the Conservatives early in the morning. Lynn Verge makes it official, she will not be a candidate. Nearly everyone wondered how she would fit back into the Tory caucus anyway, with the way Ed Byrne and Roger Fitzgerald hastened her departure in 1986. But most concede Verge would have brought star quality and energy to a questionable lineup. She will be on the team as co-chair of the campaign, but it's candidates Ed Byrne needs.

Later in the day, Byrne turns his attention to that matter, getting enough candidates to fill out the slate.

Jack Harris is meeting with organizers. This election is not a convenient one for either opposition party.

Brian Tobin has been on the road, flying here, there and everywhere. He's campaigning hard, and this is only a couple of days into the campaign. People who know Tobin, say this is how he runs — fast and hard.

I am finishing the story on unemployment. A whole generation of Newfoundlanders, including myself, have grown up with double-digit unemployment. The Newfoundland rate was last under 10-percent in 1972. It's now 18.7 and likely to increase when the numbers are released for January. A caller to the Here & Now feedback line says lack of jobs is the major issue in the campaign, although he claims you wouldn't say that when you consider what Tobin claims are the issues.

There's some serious business happening at Conservative headquarters tonight. Ed Byrne is huddling with party strategists. They want former leader, and for a brief time, Premier, Tom Rideout to run. The problem is — where? He had planned to run in Windsor-Green Bay against Liberal Graham Flight, in a district adjacent to his old seat in Baie Verte. But a local candidate wants that one. Rideout doesn't want to be seen as the old guy who doesn't know when to leave. The strategists look for a weak Liberal seat. They settle on Burgeo and LaPoile. They're encouraged by all the news about a challenge to Liberal Bill Ramsay in the nomination. That, coupled with Bill Matthews hold on the federal seat, should give Rideout a decent base. Even now though, Rideout isn't sure. He wants to wait until after Liberal nominations close on January 21 to make up his mind.

The Conservatives are disappointed about Labrador West. They have a candidate in mind, but he's not able to get the time off work to run. Candidate recruitment takes on a cold and chilling feel when you're the Opposition and behind in the polls. The Conservatives have about 30 candidates in place. There are just 16 days left in the campaign.

The Liberals will sleep a little sounder tonight. They've just put the finishing touches on nomination votes for tomorrow. All 48 candidates will be in place after tomorrow night.

Election Diary

January 21, 1999

It sure doesn't look like January on the east coast. There's not a flake of snow to be found. The Conservatives can't even blame the government for calling an election in the dead of winter.

On two stops today, Brian Tobin takes Ed Byrne to task for suggesting health care boards be dismantled and CEO's answer to the politicians in St. John's. Tobin claims this would take Newfoundland "back to the 1940's." It's not supposed to be this way. Ed Byrne should be on the attack.

A Conservative strategist tells me they've practically given up on Labrador, calling it "a desert land." He tells me how tough it is to get candidates, how everyone wants to be on the winning side. He talks about how strong Brian Tobin is in this election. He feels there may be a complacency factor with the Liberals, and asks "can Ed and the boys capitalize on it?"

The Liberals are taking every step to avoid anything that might suggest disunity, and they want to put the clamps on any infighting. They've had all candidates sign a declaration affirming they will support the Liberal candidate in the district, and promise to not seek election either as an independent or as a candidate for another political party. Executive director Fred Rowe says it's an idea they borrowed from the federal Liberals. Rowe is delighted the Cartwright-L'anse au Clair race hasn't degenerated into the "holy war" it became in 1996. He's just gotten off the phone talking to the Danny Dumaresque and Yvonne Jones camps, and "it seems to be okay." Rowe hopes "nothing happens to ruin it."

Jack Harris announced his education policy at Memorial University. Here & Now tells the story of how the NDP's supporters and friends in the labour movement are donating time and space to fund the campaign. There is no question the NDP does things differently. The party has been able to attract Randy Collins of the Steelworkers Union to run against Liberal Perry Canning in Western Labrador. He plans to run Canning into the ground because the government agrees it makes economic sense for IOCC to expand and restart a pellet plant at Sept-Isles, Quebec rather than expand its plant in Labrador City. Canning got a couple of bonus public appearances with the Premier and Mines Minister the week before the election. Will it pay off?

Election Diary

Friday, January 22, 1999

The lineup has been set for the Liberals and nearly set for the Conservatives. Last night was not a time for comebacks in the Liberal camp. One incumbent MHA — Bill Ramsay in Port aux Basques — and two former MHA's, Danny Dumaresque in Cartwright-L'anse au Clair and Bill Hogan in Placentia, were defeated in their attempt at comebacks. While I was at the Liberal headquarters this afternoon to do an interview on strategy for a party that's ahead in the polls, the Premier's chief of staff — Gerry Glavine —gushes over the fact that 12,500 Liberals voted in last night's nominations.

On the Conservative side, former leader and short-lived Premier Tom Rideout finally announces he's back. He would have chosen Burgeo and Lapoile if Liberal Bill Ramsay had made the cut. Rideout and the Conservatives figured Ramsey would have no chance of winning the district had he been the candidate. But Liberals in that district decided the issue, and placed Ramsay third out of three candidates. Rideout has opted instead for Lewisporte to face Melvin Penney. Penney won in a runoff last night, and last fall was regarded as one of the Liberals not anxious to have a September election.

When Rideout steps off the PC bus at Confederation Building with Ed Byrne to be presented to the press, he talks about the need to have a strong voice for rural Newfoundland.

Some of the most interesting people in any party are behind the scenes. Today, I get to meet two of them. Incidentally, they are former Education Ministers, one a Conservative, the other a Liberal.

I'm doing a television news segment about parties having wide leads in the public opinion polls. The question is a simple one — can a party lose a big lead?

Loyola Hearn comes to our station ten minutes before the interview. I take him to the cafeteria and get him coffee. We talk about recruiting candidates, and he reveals how tough it has been to get the candidate they wanted in Labrador West. The Conservatives have had to settle on their third choice. Interestingly, he doesn't talk in terms of winning this election. He believes the party is more ready than they have been in any election since the 1980's; that Ed Byrne is on the right side on the issues; that people will question why Tobin called a vote this soon into his mandate.

After all that, Hearn reasons, Tobin's support will begin to erode, and Ed Byrne could give Tobin a tough race.

Yes, he says, a party can lose a big lead. And Hearn was there to experience it. In 1989, the Conservatives under Tom Rideout had a 28-point lead after their leadership convention. Within a few days, Rideout called an election. Within ten days of that, support for the government began to dip. The Conservatives won the popular vote with a slight edge. But they lost the government to Clyde Wells. Hearn himself, in the safe Conservative seat of St. Mary's-The Capes, had no idea of the slide until he attended a party meeting where Conservative strategist Cabot Martin warned everyone they were losing.

The Conservative strategy in 1999 was to keep hammering away at Tobin's motives for calling an early election, and lay out for people the Conservative platform on the hot-button public issues of health and education. The emotional and always present issues of out-migration and unemployment would also be part of the Conservative plan.

Loyola Hearn insisted on being interviewed away from the party offices on Elizabeth Avenue. The Liberals had no problem with an interview in their campaign office at the Ashley Building on Peet Street. No one played up the connection, but Liberal stalwart Joe Ashley who had died in the fall of 1998, would have been proud to see his premises rented out to the party he supported for a lifetime.

Campaign chair George Furey met me and took me on a brief tour of the offices. The finance office, the tour headquarters, Furey's office. Not the luxurious surroundings The Telegram wrote about he claimed, but a rather ordinary office with — and Furey made sure I understood this — a vinyl, not leather-covered chair. Furey arranged an interview with Phil Warren, a former education professor of mine, Royal Commission chair, Liberal backroom worker, strategist, many times a candidate, finally MHA for St. John's North and Education Minister.

The setting was a long room, formerly occupied by a paint shop. This was the distribution room, as the Liberals called it. Piles of plastic board posters, boxes of the Liberal policy book piled against one wall, bags of Liberal pins. This was the machinery of an election campaign. Someone had taken the care to arrange Liberal placards against the far end wall to make a Liberal red backdrop for our interview.

Loyola Hearn and Phil Warren are a bit of a rare commodity in public life. What you see is generally who they are. Some people in both parties refer to each as the last of the good guys.

Warren tells me the Liberals would stay ahead not by hitting on the opposition, but by laying out its plan for the future. Every candidate would run as if they were behind. They would follow the leader, Brian Tobin. Tobin was doing everything he could to get on television and in the newspapers. Climbing a ladder here, giving a thumbs-up there, dancing a jig with seniors at another location. Warren was of the view this exuded energy and vitality, exactly the image Liberals wanted to portray about their policies and their government. During the interview, one of the taxi buses from out of town makes a stop to pick up posters and literature for a local candidate.

Once the distribution centre closes in a few days, Warren will hit the road and coach a few newcomers on how to properly campaign. Key among the hints — get out of the office, knock on doors, visit everyone — including people with Conservative and NDP signs in the window (but don't stop here for a cup of tea, it wastes too much time without any return!) — and never, never, knock on a door after ten at night.

I ended the day on a curious note. Loyola Hearn had mentioned to me this morning there would be a development late today or tomorrow, that would turn out to be big news. "Big news to you or to the rest of us", I asked. "To everyone," he replied.

Chapter 6

The First Week

The first week of any election campaign is a tentative time. Candidates are being nominated, their leaders are hitting the road to try their campaign message, and the public is not yet tuned into the campaign. In this environment, small pieces of news become magnified and commentators evaluate them as key pieces in the puzzle that will become the election.

One of the first apparent coups took place on the west coast in the first days of the campaign. Stephenville Mayor Cec Stein, who contested the 1996 election as a Conservative, publicly proclaimed he would vote Liberal this time because Brian Tobin was committing the government to build a new hospital in the town. The Conservatives were outraged — not at Stein, for that would likely have hurt their chances with Stephenville voters — but at Brian Tobin for having the audacity to use an issue like healthcare for the crass political motive of increasing momentum. Ed Byrne was in Corner Brook rallying Conservative candidates and supporters. He told the press: "I don't blame Cec Stein...but for the Premier to make a hospital, of all things, a bargaining chip to win the support of a local public figure is reprehensible."

For his part, Cec Stein took a back-handed swipe at Ed Byrne and the Conservatives. All the Premier did was "reconfirm" they would build a hospital he said, and besides he ran as a Conservative in the 1996 election because of his admiration for then-leader Lynn Verge. In a region where Lynn Verge is highly regarded, such comments carry weight. And they reinject the infamous Ed Byrne-Roger Fitzgerald interview into the campaign, thereby reminding people of the treatment Verge received after the 1996 election.

Tobin was doing a whirlwind tour of the west coast and northern peninsula, including his newly-adopted district of The Straits-White Bay. He toured a woodchips operation in the district, and listened to complaints that the owners needed more than $1 million to get the plant operating, and that they were having trouble doing that on their own. Tobin intimated the government would help once it received a proposal, but he also took the opportunity to slam the Conservatives' policy on assistance for business. The Conservatives, he pointed out, would cut loans and grants to business if they were elected.

This was the kind of criticism the Conservatives could do without. Many in the party, including some incumbent MHA's, believed the party's policy statement on assistance to business was not clear. In Baie Verte, Paul Shelley was pleased with the overall thrust of the policy statement, but had problems with some parts of it, including the section on assistance to business. "I had some problem with the language [in the document]. We didn't have time to fine-tune the language. We wanted to sit down over the next month before the election and fine-tune." The policy statement made it sound as if all assistance to business would end, when, according to Loyola Hearn, they were trying to say something else. We were trying to say "the time for giveaways is over, there are ways of helping business without handing out money. They weren't clear enough."

It was on the tax cuts issue though, that Byrne would take the hardest hit. He proposed a five-year phase-out of the payroll tax, and a reduction in the personal income tax. The Conservatives estimated the cost at about $500 million. This all sounded like good stuff, and the Conservatives felt it was time anyway for Newfoundland to join the national trend of stimulating the economy through tax cuts. But the Liberals lay in wait.

Finance Minister Paul Dicks was campaigning in his west coast district of Humber West when Byrne made his proposal. The Liberals were not in the tax cut game in this election, and in that environment, it simply would not do to have a Conservative promise of tax cuts on the table. Dicks received an urgent telephone call from Brian Tobin. "The Premier said you have to do something on this," Dicks recalls. The finance minister did his own rough analysis and decided to fly to

St. John's to have officials in the finance department crunch the numbers in Byrne's proposal. Not surprisingly, according to the Conservatives, the finance officials and their Liberal superiors found big problems with the tax cut proposal. Byrne realizes now, in the clear light of day, that he should have made a bigger issue of the government running to public servants in the middle of an election to bat his proposal out of the park. "I should have turned it around and said, 'how in the name of God is the public service working for the Liberal Party, explain that to me.'" Memorial University economics professor Wade Locke did a quick analysis of the proposal for *Here & Now*, and also concluded the Conservatives may have understated the cost of the tax proposal. But he claimed, the Liberals had also likely overstated the cost.

The episode carried a lesson about quick reaction and action in the context of a 21-day election, a strategy the Conservatives would later employ successfully during the Pilar Riego incident in St. John's. Paul Dicks felt it was critical the Liberals react quickly to the idea of a tax cut. "If you don't respond to it, you give the other side credibility." Dicks says the Liberals did not object to the tax cut on the grounds that they themselves did not have one in their platform. Rather, he claims it was the province's inability to afford the lost tax revenue. "If you reduce taxes," he says, "there's no guarantee [people] will spend it on something that will find its way back to the Treasury."

The national press took Byrne to task for not forcefully defending the tax cut in the face of the Liberal response. The *National Post*'s Paul Wells commented "Mr. Byrne opened with a promise of tax cuts, then stopped talking up the idea as soon as the Liberals priced the cuts at $1 billion." Byrne himself feels vindicated in the wake of the election, given that Brian Tobin has said Newfoundland would study the possibility of reducing income tax rates. "He took strips off us and the party in the election on taxes, he knew he had to move in that direction."

The election of course was about more than tax cuts. Brian Tobin attempted to cast it as a contest over leadership, namely which leader — he or Byrne — had what it took to negotiate good deals with INCO on Voisey's Bay and with Quebec on Churchill Falls. Tobin told voters he wanted to finish the job he had started. Byrne, on the other hand, believed bread and butter issues such as healthcare and education, were more important to people in the winter of 1999 than the leadership issue Tobin espoused. How the two parties came to such diametrically different views of what the election was about, became one of the real stories of the election.

The Liberals have the benefit of holding the public purse strings. This allows the party in power, and specifically the Premier, to quiz the public on a variety of issues. Through 1998, healthcare and the quality of the service, was the main issue pollsters detected among the population of the province. On the leadership question, Byrne and Jack Harris were not even close to Tobin. Pollsters and the politicians who hired them were faced with a paradox — voters approved of Brian Tobin's leadership, yet they condemned the government on the healthcare issue.

The challenge for Brian Tobin then, was how to construct an election campaign he badly wanted, without allowing it to be dominated by the health issue. Tobin and his advisors came up with a plan to announce extra spending for healthcare prior to the election, and then turn the campaign into a popularity contest between himself and Byrne and Harris. It was not "who can best deliver healthcare?", it was "who can best negotiate good deals on Voisey's Bay and Churchill Falls?"

The Conservatives knew the game the Liberals were playing. Through the fall in the House of Assembly, they had brought up numerous cases of problems with the healthcare system. The Minister of Health, Joan Marie Aylward, would admit while everything was not perfect in healthcare, the government was working on solutions, and then she would accuse the Conservatives of "fearmongering." In other words, the Opposition was the problem, not healthcare.

Ed Byrne and the Conservatives had been doing their own polling through the fall and into January. Consistently, the poll results through November, December and January showed healthcare as the number one concern in the public's mind. Education was second to that, jobs and the economy third. Voisey's Bay and Churchill Falls finished near the bottom of the list, with about 5 percent considering it their main issue. On the leadership issue, the polls concluded what the public already knew — they knew and generally liked Brian Tobin, they didn't know Ed Byrne.

Byrne says calling the election on leadership "was the right thing for him [Tobin] to do" given the Premier's personal popularity, and the public concern about issues like healthcare. And even if Byrne had wanted to, he could not fight the election based on leadership, at least not the early part. "I'm a realist...you look at the polls for what they are, no one knew who I was. We tried to harp on the issues."

The early days of the campaign created a distinction between the two leaders that few people missed. Brian Tobin looked to be having fun, climbing a ladder to shake a workers' hand here, dancing a jig with a senior there. For Ed Byrne, it seemed to be hard work, visiting nursing homes and community colleges, talking about issues like healthcare and the economy. And worst of all, he appeared to not have much fun doing it. At one point an exasperated Jack Harris of the NDP told *The Telegram* the election was "boring." " This isn't a campaign," complained Harris, "Tobin has been driving around in his bus putting on a campaign for the media." Harris too wanted the focus to be on issues, but with just one seat in the legislature, and only 17 candidates, not many people were listening. "A lot of crisis exist and we don't need a showboat election to satisfy Mr. Tobin's agenda or needs."

The first week of the campaign is not just a time for the parties to try out their themes and slogans, it's also when the candidate gets the first sense of what the electors have on their mind. For first-time candidates like Tom Hedderson in Harbour Main-Whitbourne, there is no campaign school, just the real thing. Conservative Member of Parliament Norm Doyle, whom Hedderson campaigned for in several provincial elections, accompanied the rookie candidate for two days at the start of the election. "I went to the first door and he let me go," Hedderson remembers, "then he took me aside and said 'Tom, don't go spurting off. You had about five minutes of party policy there. That's not what people want to hear. Let them ask questions on party policy. Go up and just establish a connection.'"

Even a rookie like Hedderson though, got the unmistakable message at the door. People didn't want to talk about leadership or Voisey's Bay and Churchill Falls. They would tell Hedderson "my daughter has not been able to get certain assistance concerning a student loan"; "I haven't worked for so many years"; "my son is up in Ontario."

A winter election in St. John's and parts of the Avalon, can turn out to be little more than a romp in the snow. But in western Labrador, February is cold. For Liberal candidate Perry Canning, the 1999 election was particularly bitter. "We knew we had an uphill battle," says Canning, but even he was not prepared for the strength and vigour of the forces lined up against him on the pellet plant issue. "I remember one night when I went to this guy's house, and he cursed and swore and said a lot of nasty stuff. I just took it. I went to the next house [the same thing happened]. I was cold and frostbitten. I just kept going." As far as many in western Labrador were concerned, Canning and the government could have done more to persuade IOC to enlarge its pellet plant in the town. The feeling was so strong against Canning, that he had to run much of the first 15 days of the campaign with a skeleton staff — himself, his wife Andrea, former Wabush mayor Bill Kelly and a couple of other supporters. "It was tough. I had to do a lot of the legwork myself. I had to do a lot of the advertising myself."

As he went door-to-door, and met people at events in the town, Canning recalled the mood being "difficult, people were distant. They were angry." He himself had trouble coming to grips with the fact that a close friend, Randy Collins, had decided to run against him on an issue that Canning claims they both knew was out of his control to change. Perry Canning wondered if this was reality — if this was the Labrador City he and his family had moved to from Main Brook on the Northern Peninsula in 1966, when he was just six years old. "Picture yourself, your best friends," he says. "People you drop in on and have a beer with, and socialize with. You go to the cabin together, you ski-doo together. All of a sudden you feel these people set you up and they know the difference."

In Port de Grave, Conservative Paul Cooper set a modest goal in a district he knew he could not win. "I wanted 1000 votes," he says, "I didn't want to embarrass myself or the party." Aware that most in the party considered him to be "a sacrificial lamb" in a contest against John Efford, Cooper wanted to poll a respectable number of votes to retain some level of credibility so that he can run in a future election. His own strategy in Port de Grave was to dovetail with the party's strategy of keeping John Efford in the district, and prevent him from helping Liberal candidates in the nearby districts of Harbour Grace-Carbonear and Harbour Main-Whitbourne.

Paul Cooper comes from a Pentecostal family and decided to play that card in the election. He reasoned the logical place to lay out that strategy was in the community of Port de Grave, John Efford's hometown, and a significant base of Pentecostal support. "He owns that community, that's his approach to it," says Cooper. The school board had closed the town's Pentecostal school. Said Cooper, "I was hoping to turn it into some kind of support there for me." So, one Sunday morning, Cooper went to the Pentecostal church service. Introduced to the congregation by the pastor, a friend of Cooper's family, the Conservative candidate introduced himself to a couple of hundred voters. "I knew he was highly offended," Cooper said of Efford's reaction to his decision to bring religion and schools into the campaign.

That would be putting it mildly. "Paul attacked me," Efford recalls, "one of the things he got on to right away was religion." The school in Port de Grave was suffering the same fate as dozens of others in rural Newfoundland, enrolment was in decline, and eventually, programs would be cut. "It had nothing to do with politics," says Efford, "there were 80 students, the numbers were not there to keep the school open." He was equally unamused with Cooper's decision to attend church to bring attention to the school issue and to court support. "That's something I don't do," remarks Efford. "He did that and that spread through the district."

The campaign had begun with a carefully laid plan on the part of the Liberals. Leadership was the issue they claimed, and they set out a series of election ads that presented Brian Tobin as a statesman presiding over a Newfoundland and Labrador that was undergoing change that would bring it into a new and more prosperous era. The ads, with Tobin's smooth and reassuring voice, dominated the radio and television airwaves. The Conservatives on the other hand, talked about issues and concerns. They promoted the team headed by Ed Byrne, and promised "government that works." The New Democrats promoted Jack Harris as a listener and showed him meeting and listening to ordinary people on the streets. Their concerns were healthcare and education, and they were critical of the way the government treated a range of people, including public service pensioners and civil servants. It was a distinction that could not be missed —the Liberals with their focus on a bright future under a leader who was strong and reassuring; the Conservatives focusing on the team approach and valiantly trying to remind the public of "the real issues"; and the New Democrats showing Jack Harris as an ordinary guy with a serious concern about social issues.

Elections though, have a way of finding their own equilibrium. Give the electorate a few days, and people and communities and groups find a way to focus attention on their own issues. In the 1999 vote, that combination of factors would put pressure on the Liberals to redefine some issues and react to the public's concern on others. It might not be enough to strike a mortal blow to the government, but heading into the second week of the campaign, it was enough to cause the Liberals a great deal of concern.

Election Diary

Monday, January 25, 1999

With one full week of campaigning completed, this election has started to take on shape. They're not saying it — and who would expect that — but the Conservatives appear to be having a tough time attracting candidates. Their candidate in Torngat Mountains is a St. John's boarding home owner — Pilar Riego. She ran in the 1997 St. John's municipal election with the slogan "God is my co-pilot." I'm afraid she will need more help than that, since Wally Anderson appears to be entrenched in that seat. I ask a Conservative campaign worker how Riego came to be the candidate in Torngat Mountains. "I don't know", he tells me. He informs me Loyola Hearn can tell me, since he's done a lot of the candidate searches.

It looked until today that Fisheries Minister John Efford would go in by acclamation. The Conservatives persuaded Paul Cooper to enter the race. Cooper was Hugh Twomey's executive assistant in the late 1980's. He ran unsuccessfully against Roger Grimes in Exploit's in 1993. It can't be a happy moment to put your name on the ballot against the Liberal who prides himself on having among the largest margin of victory of any candidate.

The rumours and half-truths are starting to fly. Someone calls from Conservative Paul Brown's campaign in St. John's Centre and claims supporters of their opponent, Liberal Joan Marie Aylward, are tearing up Brown's campaign signs. And they have two witnesses on Pennywell Road who not only saw the act, but could attest the sign destroyers came to their doors minutes later soliciting support for Aylward.

A source at the Liberal headquarters wonders why the Conservatives have no candidate in Grand Bank yet. There's even a second-hand report that the Conservative candidate in Cartwright-L'anse au Clair can't access party funds. The source tells me when the party can't provide funds, some candidates become disillusioned. As for Conservative Paul Hunt in Bay of Islands, I'm told he just got back from Africa. And Dan O'Brien from Gander has been in Cuba.

I've learned something else besides the rumours — the Liberals are not sure if they will send Brian Tobin into Labrador West. The steelworkers are making a big deal of the IOCC pellet plant issue, and they are unhappy with Tobin. What effect will that have on the incumbent MHA Perry Canning? The source tells me they have no feel yet for how Canning is doing.

Canning himself has circulated an 8-month old letter from George Kean of the Steelworkers. In it, Kean praises Canning as a member, and proposes he be elevated to cabinet.

There's one thing I still haven't found out. What was it Loyola Hearn promised on Friday? What big story could create news? He told me today, that one will have to wait until after the election. I can wait.

Election Diary

Tuesday, January 26, 1999

The Conservatives are finally being heard. In Springdale, Ed Byrne challenges Brian Tobin on the necessity of having an election now.

Tobin runs into demonstrators on two stops. In Port aux Basques, members of the South West Coast Development Association confront him about inattention to local problems. Liberals want to make sure everyone hears that Bill Ramsey, the incumbent MHA defeated in the nomination, was helping lead their parade around the town. This is party unity!

Thursday night, Tobin runs into disgruntled nurses in Corner Brook. They disrupt a Liberal rally.

Will this kind of demonstration snowball? Tobin and his advisors must now know the next 14 days will be tougher sledding than they imagined.

The Conservatives meanwhile, still don't have candidates in Port aux Basques and Grand Bank.

Election Diary

January 27, 1999

This is the day political leaders fear. A candidate upstages the leader and the campaign. It happens in St. John's and the Conservatives are none too happy.

Pilar Riego, the only person who wanted to contest the Conservative nomination in Torngat Mountains, had her name on the party website since last weekend. People laughed and snickered, after all, wasn't this the person who ran in the last St. John's municipal election with the slogan "God is my co-pilot"! Every campaign has its share of "amusing" candidates, and the Conservatives were prepared to accept that in this one as the price for having an open nomination system. What happened next though, they were not prepared for.

Here & Now's Natalie Clancy reported Riego had a conviction for fraud in her background. And while her cameraman was shooting pictures of Riego dishing out chicken noodle soup for her boarders, one of the boarders revealed he had signed Riego's nomination papers. And not only that, he had signed the names of several of his relatives, who were living in Labrador. Confronted with this, Riego claimed the cost of long distance charges prevented her from getting those names herself, and she promised to make things right. After the Here & Now story aired, the Conservatives called our St. John's newsroom and said Ed Byrne would not sign Riego's papers. She would not be the party's candidate.

Privately, the Conservatives are fuming. This is not the kind of story that gives a campaign momentum.

The Liberals left Port aux Basques for Brian Tobin's new district — The Straits-White Bay. Tobin finds out that problems with the Fisheries Loan Board and other local issues — carry more weight there than his tough stand on Voisey's Bay and a Churchill Falls deal. The New Democrats are following their "issue a day" strategy, today pointing out that the Liberals plan to increase rates to use the provincial ferry system. The Liberals steal the sting from that one, with a statement that says the new rates will be reviewed, and will not be implemented now.

Election Diary

January 28, 1999

New Democrats claim they are different than the other parties. It's certainly true in how they run the campaign. Jack Harris visited Trinity North today in a rented minivan — one driver, no aides. The first van they rented turned out to be red — someone made sure it was taken back and replaced. Harris could do without being needled about riding around in a Liberal-red van.

This campaign is all about the leaders. It's the way the parties present it, and the way the media covers the race.

For Harris though, this is also about his personal seat in Signal Hill-Quidi Vidi. Some are starting to say Pete Soucy, alias Snook, will give Harris a run for the money. One caller tells me people have not forgotten Harris' unsuccessful run for the mayor's job in St. John's in 1997, when it appeared he was ready to abandon the NDP for his own personal ambitions.

The Pilar Riego kerfuffle is over, and on the open lines, people have moved to another issue. NTV, which is running the television debate, has excluded Newfoundland and Labrador Party leader Sue Kelland-Dyer, from the February 1 event. The phone lines are filled with people contemplating everything from demonstrating at NTV the night of the debate, to refusing to watch the NTV Evening News. Jim Furlong of NTV stands his ground. Only the three parties with representation in the legislature will get to take part in the debate.

Chapter 7

Pilar Riego

It was not the news Ed Byrne wanted to hear. *Here & Now* reporter Rick Seaward and his cameraman Rod Dobbin had followed the Conservative leader in Corner Brook and elsewhere on the West Coast all day. Seaward had been told by the St. John's newsroom that one of Byrne's candidates — Pilar Riego — had made the startling admission her nomination papers were signed, not by people living in the Torngat Mountains district, but instead by people living in her boarding house in St. John's. Riego's Lord God Almighty Creator and King of Heaven and Earth Hospitality Inn on Bonaventure Avenue in St. John's would need all the heavenly miracles it could muster before this day was out. Pilar Riego's interview with *Here & Now* not only proved she had fraudulently obtained the signatures of residents of Torngat Mountains, she also appeared to have no idea on how to meet the needs of people who lived in the district. CBC reporter Natalie Clancy, just arrived in St. John's from Calgary, had a story, and everyone, including Byrne knew it.

The story opened with Riego and Clancy standing outside the boarding house. Riego, who had taught school in Davis Inlet 27 years before, told Clancy she knew the district of Torngat Mountains to be "a very snowy, mountainous area." It was when the interview moved inside the house, that it became apparent there was a large gap between what the Conservatives would hope to have in a candidate for the region, and what they now appeared to have.

Clancy: What are the issues there? What do the people want there?

Riego: Ah (long pause — licks finger, starts to fumble for documents off-camera) Okay, I will represent all the people of Torngat

Mountains, if I may, and they will have an honest member. Pilar Riego is my name.

Riego finished the interview, and went back to work, taking up chicken noodle soup for her boarders. Clancy talked off-camera to one of the boarders from Labrador, who told how he and a friend had signed their own names and the names of their relations in Labrador on Riego's nomination papers. This of course, is not how prospective candidates go about proving to the party they have support for their decision to stand. Clancy confronted Riego with the new information.

Clancy: Who signed all those names, your tenants?

Riego: I asked them if they knew their fathers and mothers, so we are going now to ask their permission in campaign headquarters, because I do not have enough money to pay the long distance telephone bills. So, I will go and ask their help, the PC.

Byrne's executive assistant Kim Puddister, accompanied the leader to Corner Brook's Valley Mall for some handshaking. The mall tour represents the showing of the flag and the leader that is an integral part of the modern day campaign. It is not only the people you meet at the mall who matter, but they will tell their friends and acquaintances and eventually half of Corner Brook would know Ed Byrne was there. Rick Seaward wanted to know if Byrne would be available for an interview after the Pilar Riego segment ran on that evening's television newscast. Yes, he would, Puddister told Seaward. Byrne himself told Seaward he wanted to see the television segment before he would comment.

Now, the challenge was to find out what exactly Riego had said. Puddister made a frantic call to the St. John's headquarters. They could offer no help, so all the campaign could do was watch the news like the rest of Newfoundland and Labrador.

Byrne had a busy night in front of him, having invited all the Conservative candidates on the West Coast to a pep rally. His one-time political adversary, Lynn Verge, was co-chair of the campaign and everyone felt she had worked hard to bring the campaign together. Before the meeting though, Byrne wanted to see the news.

Kim Puddister still had to see the story for herself. "We couldn't just take the reporter's word for it," she recalled. She sat down in the Glynmill Inn's Tudor Suite to watch *Here & Now* with Byrne and two other supporters.

Back in St. John's, campaign chair Loyola Hearn was watching as well. He'd been interviewed by *Here & Now* earlier in the day, and said he would also wait until seeing the newscast to make any statement. Despite Hearn's conviction that "our party is an open party," what he saw on the television news convinced him the party had to act quickly to cancel Pilar Riego's candidacy.

In Corner Brook, Ed Byrne had the same thought. "I picked up the phone," Byrne remembers, "I was mad as hell. I said phone CBC immediately. Disassociate ourselves with that."

What happened next was proof that in politics, as in life, it is sometimes possible to make a silk purse out of a sow's ear. Hearn was still on the phone with Byrne and his staff at the Glynmill Inn in Corner Brook, when someone at headquarters told him there was an important phone call. Hearn picked up the call and discovered the caller was Simeon Tshakapesh from Davis Inlet. A former chief in the community, and one of the first community constables, Tshakapesh had not heard about the kerfuffle surrounding Pilar Riego. He told Hearn he was interested in running for the Conservatives in Torngat Mountains. Hearn went through the business about getting names of supporters on a nomination form, and got off the phone thinking a little good had come out of a bad situation.

Hearn telephoned *Here & Now* while the show was still on the air. Pilar Riego's nomination for Torngat Mountains would not stand he said, and the party would soon have a new candidate. The news reached Byrne's team in Corner Brook and his executive assistant Kim Puddister could barely contain herself.

Ed Byrne went through with his scheduled meeting with west coast supporters and area candidates, a disheartening prospect considering "that everyone going to the rally was watching the news that night too." But campaigns are about boosting yourself and the party, not for feeling sorry. The PC campaign is based on "teams, not one man," Byrne declared to supporters. He promised a strong fight against Brian Tobin, and undertook to make the election a race. While Byrne rallied the troops, Kim Puddister was working to confirm Simeon Tshakapesh was indeed the Conservative candidate in Torngat Mountains. "I'm not going to tell Ed until it's confirmed," she recalls. "I didn't want to be playing with his emotions." Puddister sensed reporters gathering for the kill with her leader, and she wanted Byrne to preempt their attack with an announcement of his own.

"I remember winking at a couple of reporters and saying — hang on there now," she recalls. Byrne left the meeting and went back to his room at the Glynmill Inn. He phoned Loyola Hearn in St. John's who told him, "we've got a solution." Hearn confirmed that he had just received a faxed copy of Tshakapesh's nomination papers. Byrne went to the lobby of the Glynmill Inn and faced the throng of waiting reporters. He had no choice but to withdraw Riego's nomination, he told the press, then reopen nominations, and was now proud to say Simeon Tshakapesh would be the Conservative candidate in Torngat Mountains. Said Byrne to the waiting crush of media, "we opened up nominations tonight. We have received a nomination from an incredible candidate." Said Kim Puddister, "someone said to me — you fell 16,000 feet and lived. It could have gone much worse, we did the best we could with that situation." Byrne himself regarded the Riego incident as "a tough couple of hours."

The Liberals did not try to make political hay out of the Riego incident, but then they didn't have to. Brian Tobin would only say that unfortunate things sometimes happen in campaigns.

Chapter 8

Efford and Cooper

Reuben John Efford is surrounded in his fisheries ministers' office with things that represent, and speak of Newfoundland. On one wall, there's a picture of his home town of Port de Grave, on another a picture of Quidi Vidi Village. Another wall has a framed map of the fisheries divisions off Newfoundland and Labrador. Tables and other pieces of furniture in his office carry their share of Newfoundlandia. There is bottled water from South Brook, bottled incidentally by a young man from Port de Grave and his partner from South Brook. There's a piece of Inuit art, a bottle of protein made from seal products. On another desk there's a decorated piece of driftwood, and a sharp-looking package containing seaweed products made in Ramea. Next to John Efford's desk is the Newfoundland flag.

"Every drop of blood that flows through my veins is Newfoundland, and more particularly, Port de Grave," says Efford, settling back into the well-padded leather chair that adorns his office. The son of a fisherman, Efford has the job he always wanted in Newfoundland politics, Minister of Fisheries and Aquaculture. The road to this office though has taken him on a circuitous route through rural Newfoundland, Toronto, St. John's and back to Port de Grave.

John Efford was 16 when he landed his first job, a teaching position at Triton Island, Green Bay. Look at the map, and you will find Triton Island near Springdale. But go there by boat and you will find a deserted community, another victim of the 1960's resettlement program. John Efford did not take to teaching, so when school ended in the spring of 1961 he left Green Bay and headed home to Port de Grave.

Like generations before him, and a couple of generations since,

John Efford landed in the fishing boat. He fished with his father in the summer of 1961. Reuben Efford had fished all his life, raised ten children and kept the family going with the meagre payoff from fishing and his own vegetable garden. "You weren't hungry, but you weren't rich by any means," is how John Efford remembers it, and he got the itch to move on.

The bright lights of Toronto beckoned and 18-year old John Efford took his chance in the early part of 1962. Only half jokingly does he concede he went there to make his fortune. But Toronto's bright lights hid the truth. A young man without professional training would find a job all right, but it was a treadmill that would return little more than enough to pay the rent. John Efford settled into a job repairing office machines and photocopiers. It grated on him that the reality of work in Toronto was a nine to five grind with none of the payoff he anticipated. It did not help either that the salt air that sustained him at home, was only a painful memory.

Efford vowed to leave Toronto at the first opportunity. But he could not bring himself to call home for money. So he looked for a second job. Taxi driving appealed to him but friends said "you will never get a taxi license." John Efford navigated his way through the bureaucracy at Toronto City Hall and got his taxi license and badge. He jumped in his Yellow Cab at six every evening for nearly a year-and-a-half, staying on Toronto's streets until two or three in the morning. In late 1963, John Efford had the money he needed to pay his trip home. "I returned to Port de Grave, and I've never left since."

It would be five more years before Efford went near politics. During the 1960's, he set the seeds for a string of businesses that would leave him "not a millionaire, but I can live comfortably [without politics]."

The Newfoundland retail and wholesale business scene was in evolution during the mid-1960's. Confederation had arrived 15 years earlier and the province was undergoing a building spree. The Trans Canada Highway was near completion and roads were being put through to the various bays and previously isolated communities. This, combined with the flow of money from Ottawa in the form of family allowances, old age pensions, unemployment insurance, and other payments, all created business opportunity. The big national wholesale and retail firms were just in their infancy in Newfoundland so there was still a dollar to be made by someone with the financial backing and the drive.

John Efford had the drive but not the finances. From his job as a salesman with Royal Grocery, he wondered why he could not do the selling for himself. As he made his rounds to the various institutions and restaurants in St. John's, peddling five gallon containers of jam and other types of food products, he became convinced he could be in business himself, if only he had the money. But the banks, all of them, gave a firm no to his request for a $3000 loan to start his own wholesale business. It was a valued friendship that freed up the cash for Efford's business venture. His 10-pin bowling buddy, Bob Murray, owned a grocery business. They got to talking one day and Murray querried the 20-year Efford on how serious he was about going into business. Murray, convinced that Efford was for real, called his wife and asked her to get $3000 together as a loan to Efford. John Efford went up to the Murray's house, picked up the money and drove to Seal Cove, Conception Bay, to buy a van for his new business.

John Efford paid $600 for the van and with the rest, went to wholesaler W.E. King on Hayward Avenue in St. John's, "and bought $2400 worth of what I would call today, junk — pet food, nylons, hair nets and safety pins." He parlayed that investment into Efford's Wholesale, and later, a plumbing and heating business, and a women's clothing store. Efford sold the wholesale business in 1979, and five years later in 1984, he sold the plumbing and heating business and the women's clothing store.

By now, he was convinced he wanted to make a try at provincial politics. The sale of his business assets was part of the strategy. "I said I would never get into politics until I could financially afford it, if you lose, your family is in a hell of a position." Satisfied that his family would make it even if he bombed in politics, John Efford took on the sitting MHA, PC Randy Collins in the spring election of 1985.

"I knocked on every single door in the district and wherever there was somebody, I spoke with them," he recounts. "I wanted to let them know I would not let them down, I would live in my district, my phone number would be published, and I would be available anytime they wanted to meet with me." Efford had his work cut out. After all, Randy Collins was on the government side and the Liberals were regarded as long-shots in the 1985 election. Collins had delivered on his promise to have an arena built at Bay Roberts, and Efford conceded Collins "was the driving force personally toward getting that arena done. He led walk-a-thon after walk-a-thon to raise funds."

Efford said he refused to be critical of Collins during the campaign, preferring instead to persuade electors he would be their best hope. "You hire me," he told voters, "the same as hiring somebody for a job. It's also your right in the next election to fire me for not doing my job. That's what I said."

The voters in Port de Grave voted for Efford in that election, and have voted for him in the four elections since. He has had his share of political trouble. Clyde Wells fired him as Social Services Minister in 1991, after someone in Efford's office obtained for a candidate in a job competition, the set of questions to be used in the interview. The Opposition charged it was patronage under the guise of a wide-open competition, and Clyde Wells fired his minister. Efford made it back to cabinet after the 1993 election. He became Works, Services and Transportation Minister. He got into trouble with Wells again, having been accused of interceding with the Fisheries Loan Board on behalf of his brother Harold. Efford says Wells wanted to toss him out for good, but after a heated meeting between the two, decided Justice John Mahoney would review the matter to determine the propriety of Efford's actions. Two weeks later, Efford was cleared and was reinstated to his job. In 1996 after Brian Tobin came back to lead the Liberals, Efford was appointed Minister of Fisheries and Aquaculture, a position he was reappointed to after the February 1999 election.

The Conservatives scrambled for a candidate to face off against Efford. The job went to Paul Cooper, a native of Point Leamington, and former assistant to Health Minister Hugh Twomey in the mid 1980's. Twomey was an affable Irish doctor, whose dry wit and pleasant demeanor made him a favourite of both sides of the House.

Cooper tried taking the Exploits seat for the Conservatives in the Liberal win of 1989 and again in 1993. He was soundly beaten both times by Roger Grimes. Like his leader, Cooper questioned Tobin's motive in calling the election so soon in his mandate, and felt the "bread and butter issues" of the fishery, healthcare, education and unemployment would erode the Liberals' grasp on power.

Paul Cooper is not a guy who scares easily. He has taken on people in his own party who have made him "feel like a castoff" and he has strong opinions on everything from Danny Williams' often-touted aspirations for the party leadership ('when the rubber hits the asphalt, he's just not there') to Doug Moores' talk about running ('put some backbone in that jellyfish. Put up or shut up. Run for us next time.')

At 39, and a self-admitted political animal, Cooper has come through a lean decade, politically speaking. The Conservatives have been out of power for the whole time, and he has had to concentrate on making a living outside politics. Cooper runs a landscaping business in St. John's and claims he has worried on more than one occasion if he could meet the next Friday's payroll. But he gives the sense the business is something that tides him over until he gets a chance to break through into provincial politics.

Paul Cooper viewed the goings-on in the fall of 1998 with a great deal of interest. He thought Brian Tobin was testing the government's political strength, and that reignited his own interest in running for election. Little did he know then however, that his own journey to participating in the next election would be along a very winding road.

With family roots close to the Lewisporte district, indeed his hometown of Point Leamington was part of that district prior to redistribution, Cooper saw that as a natural area for him to test his support. As the election rumours swirled in the late summer of 1998, Cooper met with Ed Byrne and told the Conservative leader about his interest in running. His family connections in central Newfoundland told Cooper that the incumbent Liberal MHA in Lewisporte — Melvin Penney — was "weak", and that was a function of the school reform issue and the threat it formed to the concentrated Pentecostal population in the district.

Yet, when nominations were called, Cooper decided not to put his name on the ballot. His fear was "putting my name on the ballot and sitting there for months," waiting for an election call, and attempting to keep in touch with the district from St. John's. He also had his landscaping business to run, and leaving in the middle of the busiest part of the year, would be a bad decision for business. Cooper watched closely to see if anyone else would go for the nomination. "No one else ran," he says, "they [the party] made some sort of statement that the person interested was unable to put his name forward at this time because of business reasons."

Cooper went through the fall and early part of the new year thinking he had a lock on Lewisporte whenever the election would be called. What he didn't know, was that the former leader, Tom Rideout, also had his eye on Lewisporte, along with a couple of other potential seats. When the election was called, Cooper was in Florida visiting his parents. Things began to happen fast. Rideout had also been interested in running in Windsor-Buchans, but so was Ray Hunter. Hunter wouldn't back out. Another potential Rideout seat — Burgeo and Lapoile — was also ruled out at this time. He would have given strong consideration to running there against a weak Liberal incumbent Bill Ramsey. But when Ramsey lost the nomination, Rideout's interest cooled. In the midst of all of this, and with Cooper enjoying the Florida sun, Tom Rideout filed nomination papers in Lewisporte. "They gave away my seat," says Cooper. "I didn't like it one little bit." But he also admits he "hadn't made enough of a personal commitment" to running in Lewisporte, and with the election underway, the Conservatives could not afford to wait and give the Liberals any type of advantage.

With the parties already on the hustings, and Lewisporte now out of the question, Cooper asked the party how he could help. They told him there were some uncontested seats, and he could help out by running in one of those. But Cooper had already run unsuccessfully in two previous campaigns in Exploits district against Roger Grimes, and he wasn't anxious to merely "be a name on a ballot." He first looked at Fortune Bay-Cape La Hune, a seat held by Liberal Environment Minister Oliver Langdon. What made this potential match-up appealing to Cooper, was that Langdon had once taught him in high school. Cooper was also mindful that Langdon had been elected as a Conservative in the election of 1989, and a year later, crossed the floor to the Liberals. "Being the sport that I am, I would have loved to knock him off."

But Fortune Bay-Cape La Hune poses a considerable geographic challenge. Part of the district is on the east side of Fortune Bay, which is accessed through the Burin Peninsula Highway. The remainder of the district includes the Bay d'Espoir area and communities around Hermitage, Seal Cove and Harbour Breton. Cooper decided the "considerable travel challenges" were too much, and he closed the door on that district.

There was one more district that held some appeal for the Conservatives. From a strategic point of view, Port de Grave was adjacent to two Liberal districts where the party felt it might have a chance. Harbour Grace-Carbonear had been represented by Art Reid, who resigned from politics after the infamous "kitchen" remark to Conservative Sheila Osborne. Across the way in Harbour Main-Whitbourne, Liberal incumbent Don Whalen had lost the nomination to Wanda Dawe. In between these two district was Port de Grave, represented by John Efford. According to Cooper, the party felt if Efford could be kept in his own district, his influence in the two adjacent districts would be diminished, thereby allowing the Conservatives a better chance of winning one or both of them.

Cooper had some strategy of his own in mind. John Efford takes a political challenge personally. Cooper reasoned, "it's not a matter of winning with him, it's by how much. I said we will go out and create some havoc," although he reasoned there was little chance of the Conservatives winning the seat.

Election Diary

Friday, January 29, 1999

Ed Byrne has learned a lot during this campaign. In a short interview with me, he speaks forcefully, points with his finger to reinforce a point, and seems upbeat. Almost too much. I have seen this on losing campaigns before — Len Simms in 1993 was similar. The candidate appears to be too positive, seemingly oblivious to the events taking place around him. The fact is, despite Byrne's optimism, the Conservatives still do not have candidates in Grand Bank and Fortune Bay-Cape La Hune. And in several other districts, the party has had a tough time finding candidates, despite Tobin's fairly direct indications through the late fall and early January, that there would be an election.

The New Democrats aren't pretending they will have candidates in all the districts. Their fight in this election will be a strategic one. Jack Harris in Signal Hill-Quidi, newcomer dynamo Valerie Long, a long shot, but credible candidate in St. John's Centre, and Randy Collins of the Steelworkers Union in Western Labrador. One seat would be okay but disappointing for the NDP, two seats would be a big gain for the party, three would be ecstacy. No seats would be a disaster.

The NDP campaign doesn't put on the pretense of an election team. Jack Harris arrives at the LSPU Hall in St. John's to outline the party's culture/tourism strategy. There's no theme music, there are no aides holding his coat and papers, only a couple of greeters. And Jack.

The Liberals, despite their lead, are showing some concern in St. John's. Throughout the day, several of their candidates put out press releases demanding the school board set out its plans for school closures before the election. By late afternoon, there is a statement from all the Liberal candidates in the region. I ask a Liberal insider if they are worried about a backlash in St. John's on the schools question — "I think they may be picking it up a bit," he tells me, "there are some out there who feel it's an issue". It would be a bitter disappointment if St. John's, the place where the Liberals gained massive support for school reform and constitutional change, now bucked the Liberals because of fears about how the school changes will be implemented.

There are now just ten days of campaigning left. When you take out preparations for Monday's debate, there are really just five or six days of campaigning, about five days of key television coverage. Ed Byrne tells me the Liberals are starting to run scared. "They're seeing the same polls as we are," he tells me, "and they know we're on the move." The Conservatives plan to leave St. John's and campaign hard for the final few days of the campaign. They've spent most of the first part of the election around the capital city.

The Liberals are confident of victory and plan to put on a few rallies in the Tuesday to Friday section of the last week. "The government will change one time," I'm told by one Liberal, "but this is not the time."

We've reached that stage of the campaign where the preliminaries are finished. The Liberals and Conservatives, each in their own way, will now sprint to the finish.

Chapter 9

On The Doorstep

Liberal party campaign headquarters in St. John's was in the Ashley Building on Peet Street, just behind Canadian Tire. It's one of those buildings hundreds of cars pass by every day, but people give little thought to what happens inside. Joe Ashley made friends with Joey Smallwood at the time of Confederation, and his firms enjoyed considerable success in the contracting business in the post-Confederation building boom. His family enjoyed numerous political connections with the Liberal party. Ashley's daughter Isabelle married lawyer Aiden Hennebury, a former Liberal party president, whose untimely death from cancer ended what surely would have been a long career in politics. Joe Ashley's daughter, Bonnie Hickey, surprised everyone, including herself, when she got elected to Parliament for St. John's East in the Liberal victory of 1993. Joe Ashley Junior was an assistant to former Newfoundland Finance Minister Hubert Kitchen.

Upstairs, in the western corner of the building, is the Liberal Party's permanent offices. Downstairs, there is a series of rooms, some of which had been leased at various times to government agencies. One space had been a paintshop. In the winter of 1999, this area became home to the Liberal campaign.

The Tour Office was situated here, where people worked out the logistics of Brian Tobin's tour. From this office, they decided where Tobin would go in various districts, what events he would attend, and which hall would be used. The Tour Office had phone numbers of key people in the district in case Tobin needed urgent help, and they would have fax numbers where they could forward correspondence.

The Communications Office was also located in the Ashley Building. From morning to night, the people who worked there monitored the news from radio, television and the newspapers, compiling everything that related to the election or that commented on candidates or public events that might have some bearing on the election. Open-line radio shows were monitored, and particular attention was paid to anything that smacked of inconsistency in the opposition message.

The headquarters also contained the distribution centre for campaign materials. In the early days of the election, this was a busy spot with a continuous stream of visitors picking up packages of posters, placards, and copies of the Red Book for the various districts.

George Furey is an unassuming and affable man whose involvement with the Liberal party goes back to his time as a high school principal in Stephenville. He left teaching after a dozen years and went to law school. Furey's law practice is in St. John's, and since 1985 he's directed Liberal campaigns as the provincial campaign manager. Furey wasn't pleased about the impression *The Telegram* had about his office. According to the paper, George's Furey's furniture "sticks out against the aged decor" at Peet Street. They described a "mahogany-coloured leather loveseat and chair, executive desk, round table and accessories that seem plush for the surroundings."

The campaign manager and the other top guns don't just manage the campaign. Sometimes they have to manage angry and disappointed candidates who, after a few days on the hustings, have become only too well acquainted with the shortcomings of their own campaign. "They're out there campaigning hard, anything can happen," says Furey, "candidates get cranky." So how does central campaign manage those cranky and out-of-sorts candidates? "You have to listen and be courteous and realize where they are coming from," Furey says. "Generally, it's candidates who are frustrated by the way their own campaign is going." One former central campaign worker recalled handling calls from frustrated and worried candidates in the 1996 campaign. "Perry [Canning] was constantly calling. You'd pick up the phone and it was him or Graham Flight," the source says. "Everything was crucial." They would tell us "I've got to get a letter out in the district today" about some matter that had come up as an issue.

In 1996, there was one phone call that shocked practically everyone in the central campaign office. The call was from Justice Minister Chris Decker's district, The Straits-White Bay, pleading for Tobin to make a visit. Decker was under challenge from an independent candidate in the Straits part of the district, but the central campaign felt Decker was safe in St. Anthony. After all, this was a district that had voted Liberal in every election since Confederation. "We checked it out, there was no problem," said one party source. "If you send in the leader one day before the election in a district that never voted Liberal, it might send out the wrong signal to the province. You have to watch for that."

There's another story about a candidate in the 1999 election who wanted to get a letter out to constituents explaining some issue that had arisen in the campaign. "I got about one-third of them out and when the candidate was out of the office, I told people to get a garbage bag to throw them out," says the source in a Liberal campaign. "I mean, it [the letter] was only a placebo to calm the candidate down."

By week two of the campaign, George Furey was hearing back on the issues from candidates who were pounding the streets and roads of the cities and towns in the province. At least three issues were raised by constituents in St. John's, and they were not the leadership issues Brian Tobin charted out on the night the campaign started. Healthcare, education reform, and the freeze in public service pension benefits were dogging Liberal candidates all over the Avalon.

With education reform, the very school boards the Liberals had devised to take decision-making away from the politicians, were now being viewed as instruments of a perceived government strategy to close down schools without a chance for the public to have a say.

The Avalon East School Board is the single biggest school board in the province, with over 80 schools before reform, and an enrolment of nearly 33,000 students, more than one-third of all students in the province. Its schools cover the whole southeastern part of the Avalon Peninsula, as well as schools in Conception Bay South, Paradise, Mount Pearl, St. John's, and the northeast Avalon. The Board commissioned reports in 1998 to redraw school boundaries and to implement the concept of neighbourhood schools. By the fall of 1998, Board chair Kathy LeGrow was indicating that over a period of several years, up to 20 schools in the district could be closed. It became an issue of whose school, and with an election in the works, suspicious parents concluded the government was attempting to get the voting over before the matter became public.

Day after day, constituents opened their doors to Liberal candidates and hurled questions at them. Which schools would close, they wanted to know? Why was the school board report being kept under wraps? At night, when tired candidates returned to their headquarters, they phoned party headquarters and reported that voters were not interested in leadership, they wanted answers to more basic questions. "A lot of the organizers told us 'this is the issue,' it became reflected at the doors," says one Liberal insider.

George Furey figures "the secret of a good campaigner is a person who can really read what they hear from people" when they go door-to-door. And he was hearing in spades from Liberal candidates, people's concern and anger about the education reform issue.

Paula Buckle, the former Royal Newfoundland Constabulary spokesperson was considered one of the star Liberal candidates. She had a large public profile, based on her almost daily appearance in the news, reporting on investigations and promoting public safety. Buckle was up against Conservative Harvey Hodder in Waterford-Kenmount, and while he was considered one of the best organized of all the candidates, Liberals felt this was a chance for an upset. Buckle though, had decided to run in a district where parents were outraged at suggestions they would not get a sought-after high school. The entire west end of St. John's, they argued, would have to send their high school children to schools in central St. John's. "We had a great candidate in Paula Buckle," Furey says, but "she was hammered on this Beaconsfield [high school] issue." Similar things were happening to Patrick Kennedy in St. John's South, and other candidates.

In the districts, workers found the issue dominated their door-to-door meetings. Said one worker in Health Minister Joan Marie Aylward's district of St. John's Centre, "we were getting calls all the time." With half a dozen schools in her district, people wanted to know Aylward's "stand on the education issue. There were people writing letters." The source said the closer things got to election day, concern on the part of parents "heightened."

The Liberals had to find a strategy, and quick, to deal with an issue that threatened to run out of control. George Furey felt the need to do something was urgent, since the Avalon East school district affected 15 Liberal candidates. "People really wanted to see this report." He called a meeting of the area candidates, who were all worried about the impact the schools issue was having on their campaigns. Says Furey, "I suggested very strongly they get out in front of the issue and call on the school board to release the report." After a long discussion, they agreed to run a full-page ad in *The Telegram* calling on the school board to make the report public. Said one Liberal candidate, "we decided to go on the offense. If we had not, the story would have been different in a couple of St. John's districts." The decision to run the ad was made early in the week of January 25, the second week of the campaign.

That Saturday, January 26, the Liberals placed their ad in *The Telegram*. "The Liberal candidates in the Avalon East School District want to make their position clear," the ad stated. It was an attempt to put the Liberals at the front of the public call for the release of the report. The ad also pushed for a consultation process, and in an effort to disassociate the Liberals from any suggestion they wanted the report suppressed, the ad said "the Board must do its job, regardless of the election."

The release of the report solved just one problem for the Liberals. The contents angered many parents. It called for schools to be closed, for children in some cases to attend school farther from home than they had previously, and it implied more school busing if consolidation was to be achieved. The Liberals might not have been able to control the school board, as the board is an independent body within the confines and budget determined by the government, but the public still saw the government as being responsible for this confusing and upsetting turn of events.

Even after the report was released, it posed a problem for the Liberals. Many people, especially in St. John's, were unhappy about the proposed realignment of schools. The underlying concern was that it was a done deal, and there would be little or no opportunity for public consultation. The politicians were hearing that on the doorstep and in the premier's office. A week before election day, Brian Tobin allowed the media a photo opportunity in his office at Confederation Building. Surrounded by cabinet ministers Julie Bettney, Walter Noel, Joan Marie Aylward, and Lloyd Matthews, Tobin, looking relaxed in a blue denim shirt, tried to appear nonchalant as he said of the schools report and concerns it created for parents: "we'll take any and every action necessary to ensure a consensus is built."

Tobin and the Liberals knew first-hand how tough an issue school realignment had become in St. John's. In Signal Hill-Quidi Vidi and Waterford Valley, two of Tobin's "star" candidates were handicapped with the schools issue. In Waterford Valley, Paula Buckle was hampered because of the Beaconsfield issue. In Signal Hill-Quidi Vidi, Pete Soucy was saddled with an identical problem. The board proposed to close Virgina Park Elementary, a neighbourhood school. As in the west end, children would have to move farther from home to attend school.

Jack Harris, the NDP leader, worried the board's proposal would create a situation where people in Signal Hill-Quidi Vidi would vote for Soucy and against him, in a strategy best explained by the belief that a government member can do more than an opposition member. He felt this was clearly an advantage for the Liberal candidate. "It's a card and you play it," he says of the Liberals. "Elect me and I will help." Harris felt that kind of message would sell in the one-third of the district that encompassed Virginia Park, rather than his message that "the bad old government is closing our school."

Over in the Conservative camp, the hot education issue was proof to campaign manager Loyola Hearn that "Brian Tobin was completely 'out to lunch' in terms of identifying issues." Conservative candidates reported the "uncertainty" voters felt about the schools issue. People told Conservative candidates they had voted in a referendum for neighbourhood schools, and "what they're [the school board] talking about is going to end up having our kids go all over the place." Hearn says the first concern at the door was "where is my child going to go?"

The schools issue was mainly played out on the eastern Avalon, since most other parts of the province carried out their reorganization the year previous. But there was one issue that affected the entire province, and for raw, emotional appeal, there was no other issue that came close.

The Liberal government in Newfoundland and Labrador was caught in the same vice-grip as other provinces when it came to healthcare. The healthcare system in the province spends about $1 billion in public funds, and the needs continue to grow. All the while, the province's ability to fund increases does not keep pace with the demand. This situation has been made worse since the late 1980's because the federal government, which funded medicare from the beginning, began to cut back on its contribution. There is a large public debate over whether this constitutes a crisis, but all debate aside, the problems are many.

Waiting lists for specialist services, including open-heart surgery, are lengthy; some regions are without medical doctors and others don't have enough nurses; healthcare professionals leave for other provinces and the United States; salaries in healthcare, as in other areas of the public service, have been stagnant for nearly a decade. Newfoundland's healthcare system had all these problems, and some more, when Brian Tobin called the 1999 election.

Nurses were the first to engage Brian Tobin in a debate about what was happening in healthcare. Their concern was two-fold: after narrowly rejecting a tentative contract agreement in the fall of 1998, their own contract talks were not making progress, and they felt the healthcare system was at risk generally. Nurses, like teachers, have a strategic advantage when it comes to political action. They reside in almost all communities of the province, and this enhances their ability to show up at political rallies and other election events.

The nurses' strategy was worked out in a meeting in St. John's in late January. They decided direct confrontation with Liberal candidates was necessary to get their point across. The decision was made to appear outside Liberal campaign functions and raise their issues directly with Tobin, his ministers and other Liberals. In a rousing and jam-packed meeting at Mary Queen of Peace Parish Hall on McDonald Drive in St. John's on January 25, nurses' president Debbie Forward proclaimed nurses were forced into political action because the province had a government and employers [hospital boards] "who have lost their way in healthcare." The room erupted in applause and cheers — the heat in the election has just been turned up by a few degrees and the leadership issue carved out by Tobin just seven days before, was now in danger of being eclipsed by questions about healthcare.

In the districts, Liberal candidates felt the heat. Forestry and Agriculture Minister Kevin Aylward knew from his door-to-door meetings with nurses, "that support from nurses was not going to be very high." He also met with a delegation of nurses at his headquarters. Despite the rumblings from nurses about their own contract situation prior to this, and concerns generally about the healthcare system, Aylward says "it was then [during the election] that I picked up the seriousness of their issues." Those issues he says, were not talked about by the administration or the hospitals in the west coast area.

As the highest profile Liberal on the hustings, Brian Tobin ran into protest after protest. There were pictures on the front pages of newspapers, all showing nurses saying their piece to Brian Tobin. Campaign chair George Furey said the strategy to deal with the nurses had to be straightforward and simple — Tobin had to react to the nurses, promise to give them a hearing, tell them the facts about the province's financial situation, but not give in. Said Furey, "the Premier would say I want to talk to you, but I have to tell you up-front, everyone else settled for 7 [percent wage increase], 7 is all we can give. Maybe we can talk about other things."

John Efford, who takes pride in knowing what's happening in his district, was taken by surprise the night Tobin attended a rally at Ascension Collegiate in Bay Roberts. Efford and Tobin were having a cup of tea in a nearby home when they noticed flashing red lights in the school parking lot. Brian Tobin, who does not like to be surprised, asked "who are those guys?" Efford, unaccustomed to being challenged in his district, mistook them for supporters. By the time the two politicians and their supporters reached the parking lot, they discovered the "supporters" to be "a few ambulance drivers and a couple of dozen nurses." Tobin defused the situation, and invited the protesters in. Efford claims some of them did come into the school, but he acknowledged "the issue was alive, the nurses were angry."

Sometimes an issue in an election can help define the campaign itself. The healthcare issue had that potential, but it did not go all the way, largely because of how the Liberals, and especially Tobin, handled the hot potato it had become.

At the start of the campaign, the Liberal ads had a "feel good" mood to them. Re-elect a Liberal government, the ads suggested, and things will stay on an even keel. But the healthcare issue in particular had shown itself to be a prickly and stubborn point of contention with the voters. With barely ten days left in the campaign, the "feel good" Liberal ads were supplemented with new ads, showing the Premier and ministers deep in conversation about issues such as healthcare. Without admitting it, the Liberals were now acknowledging healthcare was an issue, and their message was about a government that cared.

The Conservatives claim the ads were part of a frantic attempt by the Liberals to keep the lid on the healthcare issue. They suggest the Liberals' early campaign ads were put on the shelf, and new caring and listening ads were produced to inundate the airwaves. Ed Byrne says the last-minute flurry put Newfoundland's production community to the task. "You could not find a camera crew or a production crew in this province, because they were all in Corner Brook with Brian Tobin."

George Furey rejects the picture of a frantic Liberal campaign team pulling old ads from the airwaves and replacing them with new ones. But he does admit every campaign has its issues, and a political party has to react. "Not everything you see is put in the can in the first week," he says.

It wasn't just the new healthcare ads that the Conservatives had to contend with. Brian Tobin was showing himself to be equal to the groups that confronted him. Tobin was shown almost nightly in the television news wading through groups of nurses. Sometimes they yelled statements at him, at other times they engaged him in conversation. His approach was the same. He would listen, tell them he understood their concerns, then suggest it would be possible to talk about the issues after the election. It was a disarming approach and it worked.

Tobin himself believes it is an approach that not only works with the group a leader comes in contact with, but with the broader public watching on television, listening on radio, or reading about such exchanges in the newspapers. "The public is constantly underestimated," he says. "We always make the mistake of assuming that the froth of public discourse [confrontations, open line call shows, nasty letters to the editor, scuttlebutt] is what runs deep in public opinion. I think we're mostly wrong." The strategy Tobin uses to combat that type of display "is to challenge and invite a debate." His audience is not necessarily the one person he's talking to on an open line radio show, or the people who challenge him in a meeting hall. "Even if the person you're talking to continues to disagree with you, the 50 people around you who are listening, will 9 times out of 10, respond to reason. The people listening on television that night will respond to you. The people in the room will respond to you. It doesn't matter that you've lost the discussion with the person with whom you've had the debate."

Another issue led to some frantic activity in a couple of St. John's districts mid-way through the campaign. Liberals got wind of a public relations campaign emanating from St. John's City Hall. Through inquiries with sympathetic officials at City Hall, they were able to determine Mayor Andy Wells and Deputy Mayor Marie White had persuaded fellow councillors to allot a small budget to determine where St. John's candidates stood on certain issues. It was a continuation of a dispute that had been carried out months earlier between the city's mayor, Andy Wells, and St. John's cabinet ministers, principally Lloyd Matthews and Joan Marie Aylward. Wells thought the province should be paying a larger grant to the city as a substitute for property tax, and that the province should force amalgamation of Mount Pearl and the urban part of Paradise with the capital city.

Matthews was especially concerned, not so much because of the campaign, but because he believed deputy mayor White was thinking of running for the Conservatives in his district of St. John's North. Said one Liberal, "Matthews was out of his mind wondering what to do." He believed the campaign was an effort on the part of White to establish her credentials and smash his chances of reelection in the process. One source familiar with both campaigns said it took several precious campaigning days for Liberals to deal with the issue.

By February 2, city politicians were on the defensive about their $30,000 campaign. "There is no intent here to de-elect the Liberals," deputy Mayor White told *The Telegram*. "If we're not here to represent the interests of our own residents, then why are we here?"

The strategy the Liberals adopted was to place a full page ad in *The Telegram* and give city voters the province's side of the dispute. In it, the Liberal candidates asked for the support of city residents "to ensure that the City of St. John's is treated fairly and that its residents enjoy the benefits they deserve." The ad noted that 15 percent of the city's revenues came directly from the provincial government, and that in the 1996-1998 period, "over $300 million was invested" in St. John's through the Janeway and other healthcare projects, the Outer Ring Road and the Civic Centre. And in her district of St. John's Centre, Joan Marie Aylward had a letter written to be dropped in every mailbox in the district.

Matthews and Aylward were feeling the heat in what were thought to be two close races. Said one campaign official, who has worked on Liberal campaigns since the 1980's, "when you're that far into the campaign, you can take a candidate and throw them into a bag and put them in the basement because they are of no use to you. All they do is upset people in the campaign because they are emotional."

As the days went by though, it was not Marie White, but Ray Andrews who entered the race to challenge Matthews. Since his retirement from the public service, Andrews has been doing contract work on fisheries policy for the new territory of Nunavut. He was in the territory the day the election was called, and did not return to St. John's until several days later. Andrews campaigned hard, and even circulated a letter of support from his former boss, John Crosbie. Ed Byrne intimated the pressure had been on Andrews several weeks before to publicly announce he would go for the St. John's North seat. But he says, Andrews could not make the commitment then, and as a result, he lost valuable time at the start of the campaign.

The Liberals though, felt Andrews was able to capitalize on a third issue that was provincial in scope, but more concentrated in St. John's because of the large number of retired civil servants. Public service pensions had been frozen for nearly a decade, and pensioners felt it unfair that their meagre benefits were still frozen while active public servants had just obtained a 7 percent increase over 39 months. The Liberals also considered pensions "a major issue" in Walter Noel's Virginia Waters district, and considered it a major contributing reason to having reduced his majority from nearly 1300 votes in 1996 to just under 700 in 1999.

As the campaign went through the second week, a drama of sorts was playing itself out in Labrador West. Perry Canning was fighting for his seat and battling public reaction on the pellet plant issue. The dilemma for Canning and the Liberal campaign was whether Brian Tobin would go into Labrador West to help bolster Canning's campaign. Canning himself steers away from saying the Liberal strategy was to keep Tobin away from the area. "I felt it was important personally for me to face this because this was my community," says Canning. "I talked to headquarters at the time and he would have come had I asked him." But Liberal insiders say their strategy in the early part of the campaign was to keep Tobin away from the area "because the candidate felt he would like to do it on his own. It was difficult to try and get an idea how best to help Perry."

Campaign manager George Furey, and Canning himself, say Tobin had firm plans to go to the district late in the campaign, but the first ministers' meeting on healthcare intervened. Said Canning, "my time slot was pretty much during the time he was in Ottawa."

Still, other Liberals doubt if Tobin would have risked going into Labrador West. "If Brian had gone in, all it would have done was fire up the issue," said one candidate. "He would have been on television where you have demonstrators meeting the Premier. If I were in charge of the campaign, I would think long and hard before sending the Premier in there." Another candidate agreed that while it might have been Canning's call, a visit from Brian Tobin would surely have taken attention away from the Liberal campaign. "If you bring in the Premier or a certain minister, it might have flared up. It would give the union, or some of the union membership, a chance to protest."

Canning himself wanted to get voters to focus on his accomplishments. He ran two large ads on February 1 in *The Aurora*, the area's weekly newspaper. One ad counted 34 things Canning had accomplished as their member, including that he was a "proud member of the team that successfully negotiated a $340 million deal in 1997 that will be used to construct the Trans Labrador Highway." Canning proposed a "growth agenda for Labrador West." He noted the $12 billion Churchill Falls project "will create thousands of jobs," and he publicized a "comfort letter" from the Iron Ore Company to its workers that would protect all the current jobs with the company in western Labrador.

The second week of the campaign was proof that while the legislature had been dissolved for the calling of an election, ministers continued to use their position to churn out press releases and announcements. While ministers retain their position as members of the cabinet during elections, it can be argued that does not give them the right to make political announcements on behalf of their departments. Yet, that is what several ministers, including the Premier did during week two.

There were a couple of announcements that could be regarded as necessary and in the public interest. Emergency repairs to the roof of a seniors' complex in Corner Brook during a weekend of heavy rains fit into this category, and so did an "investor alert" from the government on so-called "Ponzi Schemes." But several were announcements of government funding for particular projects or programs, an apparent clear use of the machinery of government to further the interests of the Liberal Party in an election. Health Minister Joan Marie Aylward had a part in two of the announcements, giving rise to suggestions this was a strategy to enhance her profile in St. John's Centre, given that Aylward was in the middle of a tight race for her seat.

The week started with Chuck Furey urging federal fisheries to release its salmon management plan. That was followed up by Premier Tobin and Joan Marie Aylward announcing a three-year $900,000 anti-smoking campaign aimed at young people. That same afternoon, Rick Woodford announced a freeze on ferry rates on provincially-run ferries. The next afternoon, Joan Marie Aylward was in the news again. She had $710,000 to send to regional health care boards to be used in providing mental health services to 16 and 17 year olds. There were still three more announcements that day.

Chuck Furey released plans for marking the Viking 2000 celebrations; Brian Tobin announced a doubling of the tourism budget for 1999; and Julie Bettney, the Human Resources and Employment Minister, announced several "initiatives" to help social assistance recipients. They would be allowed to receive the first $500 of an income tax refund without having that money taxed back by social services, and families that moved from welfare to a job would be permitted to keep their drug card for a period of six months, rather than the previous three.

Election Diary

Monday, February 1, 1999

This is debate day, so the leaders, except Jack Harris, are being kept away from the media.

I've spoken to a couple of Liberals today about their campaign. One tells me the party is confident about their polling numbers in rural areas, but they are keeping their St. John's polling numbers "close to their chest." This information comes as the City of St. John's launches an advertising campaign posing questions for politicians about the province's financial relationship with the city. This is a thinly veiled continuation of the Mayor's war of words with the Tobin government. Andy Wells feels the city is being poorly treated, and he wants that to be an election issue.

Wells told me in early January the Conservatives should have decided to take up the issue, that this would have guaranteed that party most of the city's seats. So far, the Conservatives are sitting on the sidelines on this one. No one it seems, wants to get too close with Andy Wells.

There's a sign or two the Liberals are feeling some heat in the city. All 15 candidates for districts under the Avalon East School Board, a board that serves fully one-third of the province's school population, have taken out an ad in The Telegram asking the Board to get on with its school consolidation program. There does seem to be something to the talk I picked up late last week that Liberals are hearing about this issue on the doorstep, and more importantly, they're being stung by criticism they are behind the board's decision to hold on to the report until after the election

I heard a curious Liberal ad on radio this morning. Tom Moore, Liberal candidate in St. John's West, said "since it appears there will be a majority Liberal Government," elect a member of the government in St. John's West. It had a ring of desperation. Moore is running against Conservative Sheila Osborne, whose profile was heightened considerably in the wake of the kerfuffle in the House last fall, where the Municipal Affairs Minister, Art Reid, resigned in the wake of his comments that "she should go back to the kitchen, where she came from."

Chapter 10

The Debate

The debate is many things to many people. For opposition parties, it's the chance to prove their leader is capable of standing on the same stage as the Premier. More than that, if they are lucky, a sharp retort can inject spark into the campaign. For the Premier, it's the chance to show he's in command of the issues. If the Premier doesn't trip or get trapped, he's considered to have been the real winner of the debate.

Jack Harris had been campaigning around St. John's in the days prior to the debate, but Brian Tobin and Ed Byrne had been on the road. Cable Atlantic, Danny Williams' St. John's-based community station, made its studio available for the party leaders to get used to the lights and the studio situation they would face in the debate at NTV. Brian Tobin and Jack Harris took the cable station up on the offer, but the Conservatives were skeptical.

Loyola Hearn sent a couple of party officials to the studio on Kenmount Road to get their assessment of whether Byrne should attend. "They had a short look," Hearn says, before returning to headquarters and recommending Byrne not go. Danny Williams was felt to be a little too cozy with Brian Tobin, and Cable Atlantic's general manager, Dean McDonald, has been appointed by the Premier as chair of Newfoundland and Labrador Hydro. The people who visited the studio told Hearn of their concern that "in a lot of stations, you don't know who's on your side. You don't want to give away any secrets

Ed Byrne had been on the road for nearly two weeks by the time the debate took place. His was a two-pronged mission — persuade people to view the election through the issues the Conservatives had laid out, and convince an apparently skeptical public that he was mature enough to be their Premier. He arrived back in St. John's to prepare for the debate, convinced it wasn't the issues he needed to be coached on, but how to deal effectively in the debate with Brian Tobin.

Sunday afternoon, the day before the debate, Byrne sat down with a group of "older hands and young turks" to map out a plan for the debate. The officials had already been there for a couple of hours mulling over the issues and concerns, and attempting to come up with a game plan for the debate. What happened next persuaded many in the room that Byrne had grown during the first two weeks of the campaign. Having settled into his chair, Byrne looked around the room. Those who had gathered began to brief the young leader on party policy. Byrne held up his hands, and asked "what do you mean? I don't need a briefing on policy." He then went on to tell the roomful of supporters that "if I don't have it [policy] now, forget it. It's just as well for me to go home." The chatter stopped and Byrne told them he wanted to talk about strategy, "how to bring him [Tobin] in, how to button him down." Byrne and the rest of the group talked for several hours after that, watching Brian Tobin on videotape. What stuck out was Tobin's "offensive style" in a debate, how he will "see an opening and go after it." Byrne concluded after the long discussion, "if you can get Tobin in a situation where you press him, he will get flustered."

Former Conservative leader Len Simms, who was also co-chair of the party's campaign along with Lynn Verge, headed the debate team. Said one party member, "we put him [Byrne] through his paces with questions. He really impressed us internally," said one of the people present at the preparation. "We had a true sense he could take on the Premier."

It's not only the questions and answers that debate coaches must consider. This is preparation for a television debate, not a newspaper or radio debate. Looks count, and appearance is a big part of looks. In order to see how Byrne measured up, they videotaped his performance. Byrne was also coached on what to wear for the debate. "There's a preparation that's done from what tie is worn, to what suit, to how his hair is worn," said one party member. Byrne was sent on a shopping trip "to a professional clothing shop here in town to give him a good image of something that was new and fresh. So we wanted to project the image of the energetic, sharp-dressed individual."

All three leaders made a stop at one of St. John's finest men's clothiers, Byron Murphy of Byron's. It's not just a question of new clothing for the debate, the ties and shirts especially have to be up-to-date, and the black or blue [nothing else has power written over it!] suits are of the latest design and cut. In order to avoid gawking by other customers, arrangements were made to carry out fittings at the store after-hours.

Brian Tobin has survived more than twenty years in politics, and he knows how to stage a campaign. His style is to run, and then run some more. Liberals talk of the 1984 Mulroney sweep when Tobin held on to his Humber-St. George's-St. Barbe seat in the face of the Conservative tide. In fear of losing his seat, Tobin ran his Conservative opponent off his trail, and kept the riding for the Liberals.

He too arrived back in St. John's the day before the debate. Even with a candidate of Tobin's experience and savvy, Liberal campaign chair George Furey says "you live in fear" that there may be a major mistake. "You've got to remember these people [the leaders] have gone through a very intense time, they have everything on the line." Furey says it is more so for the government than the opposition. "If the leader of the opposition makes a faux pas, he lessens his chance of getting the Premier's chair," says the campaign chair, but "the person who is in government obviously has the most to lose. If that person makes a faux pas, he could be kissing his government goodbye, and his tenure as Premier of the province goodbye."

Furey says the preparation of the leader for the debate is "fairly intense. We set up a structure that puts him under the gun." To prepare Tobin, the Liberals had two people as stand-ins for New Democrat leader Jack Harris and Conservative leader Ed Byrne. "We gave him quite a grilling," says Furey, "you never have to worry about a seasoned campaigner and debater like Brian Tobin, but it's one of those things that's never over until its over."

It turned out that George Furey's brother, Chuck, stood in for Ed Byrne. As a cabinet minister, Furey was aware of all the internal debates on the major public issues, and he used that to his advantage to give Tobin a strong practice session. Said one source, "he [Furey] had an intimate knowledge of issues that Ed Byrne wouldn't have. He gave Tobin a run for his money." When Tobin answered a question in a particular way, Furey would come in with a counter argument that had probably been raised in a cabinet or committee meeting. "Furey was the most effective preparer I've ever seen," said one of the people present. The Liberal Tour Director, Dennis Brown, who had played Len Simms and Tom Rideout in previous debates, played NDP leader Jack Harris in this one.

The debate also featured a mock panel of journalists. Social activist Penney Rowe, who had played former Conservative leader Lynn Verge in the 1996 mock debate, played the part of a journalist. A gallery of about ten people watched, including the debate co-ordinator Ed Roberts, and Brian Tobin's wife Jodean. Their job was to critique Tobin's performance, to point out "the strengths and weaknesses." And like Byrne, Tobin had assistance on what colours to wear for the debate.

Unlike his first Newfoundland campaign in 1996, Tobin was allowed to rest on the day of the 1999 debate. In his first election, the Liberal campaign scheduled two events. One of them required him to spend part of the morning at Signal Hill with federal Heritage Minister Sheila Copps to mark National Flag Day. Later, they had him pounding the pavement in St. John's South to support Tom Murphy, a campaign Murphy lost. Tour director Dennis Brown says public appearances have to be kept to a minimum, because "the leader at that point is quite often tired, the debate is stressful. You try not to schedule too much."

Jack Harris spent part of the day of the debate in the relative solitude of his office at NDP headquarters. "I don't see it as a boxing match," he said of the anticipation of what might transpire at the debate. Like Ed Byrne, Harris felt the mental preparation for the debate was the key in the hours leading up to the debate. "A lot of it is getting yourself in a mental state to where you are comfortable with what the set is like [the TV debating studio], where you are going to be standing, where you're not trying to adjust to these things at the same time as you're trying to keep your mind focused" on the debate itself.

The debate itself, as is often the case, was an anticlimax. Tobin did not falter; Byrne made his points but didn't harm Tobin; and Harris, although steady, was a sideshow to the main event.

Chapter 11

The Media

Jay Callanan has been around Newfoundland's print and television media since the late 1970's. He was assigned by CBC Television to the first half of Brian Tobin's campaign and the second half of Jack Harris's campaign.

Peter Walsh has been a television reporter since the mid-90's. He covered the last half of Ed Byrne's campaign for *Here & Now*.

Journalists are both appreciated and cursed by election campaigns and leaders. But they are necessary. The media is the link, however imperfect, between the leader and the public. It is the press corps that reports what the leaders say, what they do, and how they do it. It is not a complete record of the campaign and its issues, but it does more than any other campaign activity to give the electorate a feel for the mood and moment of the campaign.

That is something political parties have come to understand, if not to appreciate. Seats are made available on helicopters for reporters and cameramen, hotel rooms are booked, and space is made on the campaign bus. But that isn't all. Campaigns arrange their major events of the day so radio reporters can feed items to their newscasts and television reporters can get pictures to their newscasts at night.

Peter Walsh thought he saw the real Ed Byrne on the softball field during a charity game in the summer of 1998. With the election winds blowing, the Conservative leader went up to bat against Brian Tobin, the man he would later do battle with during the real game. Byrne got a hit and reached base safely. His combined Opposition-Media team moved him along the bases and the thirty-something leader scampered home. It was only a charity game, but in answer to Walsh's question, Byrne admitted it felt good to get a hit off Tobin.

As the Conservative campaign bus rumbled up the northern

peninsula highway toward Rocky Harbour one dark night in the late stages of the campaign, Byrne and Walsh chatted easily. His jacket off, Byrne sat back, relaxed, his shirt collar and shirt cuffs undone. "I look him right in the eye," Byrne said of the times when he has had to shake hands with Brian Tobin. "When we shake hands, we do it really hard. You can't [intimidate] me." Byrne felt Brian Tobin had done just that to Lynn Verge in the 1996 election in an infamous scene at the paper mill gate in Corner Brook. Tobin took Verge's hand, practically held her in a vise-grip and proceeded to talk over the Conservative leader. Byrne had seen the episode and vowed "Tobin knows he can't do that to me." Walsh came away from the conversation that night with the impression "nothing like that would happen to him."

Brian Tobin is a campaign manager's campaigner. When things look bad, as they sometimes did in the campaign, Tobin was able to turn the event into a golden moment. He did it time after time during the 1999 campaign, converting an anxious moment into a political opportunity that called on the protester to understand the Premier's position. Jay Callanan saw such a situation develop several times in his ten days on the Tobin tour. Pensioners, nurses, and unemployed loggers came out to vent their frustrations about their issues.

During a tour of the province's biggest hospital, the Health Sciences in St. John's, Tobin was bringing some attention to healthcare and highlighting his government's attention to the issue. Dollars might be short, but he wanted to show how the expansion to the hospital's cardiac care ward, and the construction of the new children's hospital, underpinned his administration's commitment to healthcare. As he moved to the cafeteria shaking hands, "20 to 25 nurses came after him, they came out of nowhere," Callanan recalls. Embroiled in a bitter contract dispute with the government for more pay and better working conditions, they wanted to know "what will you do for us?" Tobin listened for awhile, as he did in similar situations — "he would let them vent their frustrations." Then he moved into the now-familiar routine to reporters, who had followed him through other such encounters. "He would say, 'let me ask you a question,' and from then on he had them. He had them almost on the defensive." The basic line was "we'll do what we can. But you have to understand, we're in the middle of an election now." Said Callanan, "we could tell when it was going to happen."

It happened numerous times in the campaign, and considering elections are among the infrequent times leaders will venture into shopping malls and other public places, individual voters will take the opportunity to button-hole them. On one such occurrence in Lewisporte, Tobin was touring with incumbent Melvin Penney, and whirling from one person to another, saying hello and just generally being seen. Tobin's eyes glance about in such situations, searching out one more person to approach. As he did so, he heard a person call out "Premier!" It was a situation that typified his approach and strategy to dealing with pointed questions.

Man: I'm a logger. What are you going to do to keep our jobs for us?

Tobin: What should I do?

Man: Stop the harvesters [machines that cut and harvest logs] from coming in.

Tobin: Stop them altogether?

Man: Limit them. Keep the work we got.

Tobin: If you're saying to me — and I think you're saying to me — you can't turn the clock back — we don't move the harvesters out — we'll work with you on that.

Man: You'll help us out on that?

Tobin: We'll help you out on that. If you said to me I have to take all the harvesters out and get rid of them all — if I told you that, I know you wouldn't believe me.

The conversation took 61 seconds. Tobin had avoided a confrontation; he was pleasant and not provocative; he quickly got a fix on the man's concern; he found out what the logger thought the solution was and made sure the man understood what it could not be; then he promised to be supportive under those conditions. A potentially loud and difficult confrontation was avoided, another handshake took place, and Tobin strolled on down the mall, spreading good cheer and good vibes. This approach may not work with everyone, but it is as good a ploy as any politician can muster on the spot. It appeals to people's sense of fair play, it does nothing to raise the temperature of the debate, and it always holds out the promise of some future action that will take place away from the "politics" of elections.

Reporters and politicians find themselves in close quarters for the election, traveling in the same bus, staying in the same hotel, flying on the same helicopter or airplane. They have the opportunity to observe each other, and in the case of the politicians and their staff, the chance to register direct feedback on stories they don't like.

One such situation developed while Jay Callanan and cameraman Kevin Harvey covered a demonstration by nurses outside a Liberal rally in Corner Brook. Callanan estimated 200 nurses turned out for the event. The next day, in an nonconfrontational but unsubtle way, Tobin's executive assistant Heidi Bonnell "wondered where I got the figure." The message was straight forward enough, the Liberals didn't feel there were that many demonstrators and reporters should learn how to do a better headcount. Said Callanan, "they had someone in the entourage keep track of what was on TV that night, what radio had on, what the newspapers printed."

As the campaign moved on, there was a kind of unease in the Conservative camp. Sure, party insiders were saying a good showing would be 16 seats, but they really wanted to be the government. The Conservative campaign, on the road and in head office, wanted desperately to get out the results of a poll commissioned by the party late in the campaign. Peter Walsh, who was with the tour, says he was constantly faced with subtle pressure to focus on the results of the poll which showed the party 7 to 8 points behind the Liberals. "I got the line there, this poll confirms what our internal polling was saying all along. I was getting that big time." The campaign printed up copies of the poll results and "were handing it out everywhere, to reporters, to party members."

Reporters constantly find themselves surrounded by "spin" during elections. Spin can best be described as the effort by a proponent or opponent to put an event in the best or worst possible light, depending on *their* needs at that point in the campaign. Heading into Port aux Basques at the start of the campaign, Brian Tobin was anxious to show that while incumbent Bill Ramsey lost the nomination to Kelvin Parsons, this was nothing more than a proper exercise in democracy. There were no hard feelings in Liberal land.

Journalists and their news editors and producers wanted to find out for themselves. It would certainly be a storyline that Liberals in Port aux Basques were divided enough that they canned the incumbent in a nomination fight. As the helicopters neared Port aux Basques that morning, the Liberals had a surprise for journalists expecting a juicy story. Says Jay Callanan, "the story we wanted to do was the fact that Bill Ramsey had been thrown out in the nomination. Yet, the first person, or one of the first to meet him [Tobin] was Bill Ramsey." The Liberals had anticipated the obvious storyline, and cleverly taken it away from reporters.

Things don't always work out so well for politicians, and they're left to cope with, or make the best of a situation in front of the press. One such situation occured to Ed Byrne in Labrador City. His candidate — Susan Whitten — got in place late in the campaign, and no one gave her a chance to take the seat. Byrne paid a visit though, and one of the events on his schedule was a meeting with student leaders at the community college. Recalled Peter Walsh, "it fell flat. He walked down the hallway and saw there was no one there." In its own small way, this was a test for Byrne. "He took control, he said fine, let's go to the seniors' home," says Walsh. "I respected him for that. He didn't openly show any frustration."

Ask any reporter in a close campaign, and they want to be with either the leader or the challenger. In a runaway, and that's pretty much how the 1999 vote turned out, despite the fact the Conservatives gained seats, reporters would just as soon stay with the leader. A winning campaign has a dynamic feel — the tour moves smoothly, the rallies are well-attended, and even in the absence of a strong story, there's a feeling of motion. In a losing campaign, there's an atmosphere of lethargy and contrived energy, and perhaps a little too much belly-aching on the part of the people traveling with the campaigns. Reporters who traveled with the Conservatives though, detected a fair level of support in the public, that while it never caught on fire, appeared to be evidence the party would make some gains.

The Liberal and Conservative campaigns were two different beasts in 1999. "The energy was there," recalls Peter Walsh of the Conservative campaign, but "Ed Byrne only ventured to Conservative headquarters and Conservative organized events, he didn't wade into masses of public at malls or anywhere there was a public event." Byrne's entourage consisted of himself, executive assistant Kim Puddister and Dave McCarthy. "I was amazed at how small it was," says Walsh. "I had this image it would be packed out with computers and people." The press corps consisted of CBC television and radio and *The Telegram*. What did strike Walsh was the youthfulness of the Conservative road team, including Byrne. "It struck me they were young, late 20's and early 30's. I found it interesting to see they were calling the shots." It was also obvious that the campaign had to spare its pennies. Byrne flew to some places, but mostly the campaign traveled by bus. Only late in the campaign, did they plan to use a helicopter to buzz into several districts to create the 1999 version of the old whistle stops politicians used to make by train.

The Conservatives were both envious and a little jealous of the resources available to Brian Tobin. Says Walsh, "the spin I was getting — Brian Tobin has all the money — two buses, a chopper all the time. He's not in touch with the people. We've got one bus and he's [Byrne] talking the issues all the time." But still, the Conservatives were anxious to get Byrne into a helicopter. Chris Breen [the tour director at party headquarters] was telling Walsh they had to get Byrne into the air. Weather ruined the chance to do that on a couple of days, and when they finally took to the air, the spectacle puzzled Walsh. "We were blowing in and blowing out," he recalls, of the 9 or 10 whistle stops from the west coast to the east coast. ""As someone new to the whole thing, I didn't understand what the point was. He'd drop down, shake the hand of the local candidate, say hi to a few local volunteers with the association, and then he was gone again." Says Walsh, "I guess it was to stir up vibes [in the community]. The chopper flies in. It looks great. The chopper landing. [People saying] hey, what's the fuss down there on the wharf. My God, there was no communication. There were times he barely left the earshot of the helicopter. He barely showed his face, then he left."

If Ed Byrne's campaign was slow, Brian Tobin's was on warp speed. "It was difficult to keep track of where you went with Tobin," said Jay Callanan. "He had a chartered plane at the ready on a daily basis." From Stephenville on the first day, the Liberal tour went by helicopter to Port aux Basques, then to Corner Brook by air, and on to Roddickton and Englee by helicopter. The tour moved back to Deer Lake, took a plane to St. John's, and then moved back out to Gander, by helicopter to Harbour Breton and back up to Lewisporte, Botwood and Bishop's Falls. "You were pretty much always on the go with Tobin," recalls Callanan.

The Liberals also had two campaign buses, one for the east coast and the other for the west coast. This came about after the 1996 election when drivers found it nearly impossible to move quickly enough from one coast to the other. The breaking point came when a driver, rushing to meet the tour, was stopped by the RCMP and issued with a speeding ticket in Terra Nova National Park. This election, the bus company told the Liberals, they would enforce the legal daily limits on the hours a bus driver can be on the road. The Liberals had lots of money, so a second bus was not a big issue. In fact, just before the campaign, the second bus caused the Conservatives to puzzle over when exactly the election would be called. The bus was photographed by a *Western Star* photographer outside a Corner Brook hotel. Not knowing the Liberals had a second bus under wraps at a warehouse at Donovan's Industrial Park in Mount Pearl, Conservatives figured that while an election was imminent, it might be Tuesday, not Monday, that Tobin would make the call.

The buses belonged to DRL Coachlines. Regular side-by-side seats extended about two-thirds down the bus, the remaining regular seats were removed, and replaced with a couch, coffee table, and a few plush chairs. Jay Callanan and the other reporters would sit up-front, making notes and trying to write scripts and stories on their laptop computers. One difference with Byrne's campaign, was that Tobin was often accompanied by several members of the mainland press. On long rides, Tobin would often come up to the front of the bus. Says Callanan, "he'd talk to us about kicking smoking, playing golf, losing a bit of weight, how your family was." At other times, the bus was used as a meeting place for the local MHA. Callanan says reporters would overhear bits of the conversation — "oh yes, we'll win this one hands down — no doubt, some of it would be said for us to hear."

The Liberal buses were outfitted to serve as offices on the road. 1996 was the first election where they used satellite phones, a development that allowed Tobin and his staff to call headquarter or anywhere else from the road. It also enhanced privacy. The bus was outfitted with portable faxes and laptop computers. Aides on the tour would alter the standard campaign speech and add local details. Said Callanan, "his team might say this is an issue that might come up today, or you'll be giving this speech three times. We will be in Harbour Breton. You might mention the fishplant."

The portable faxes allowed the campaign to receive press clippings and transcripts of all the radio and television news stories. That kept Tobin in touch with events away from the campaign, and gave him the opportunity to comment on issues in a timely way.

While the Tobin campaign was constant motion, the NDP campaign was "gee, what are we going to do now?" That's how Jay Callanan described his move to follow Jack Harris with 10 days left in the election. "The day wasn't long enough for Tobin, it was much, much, much too long for Jack." As Callanan and cameraman Rod Dobbin followed Harris, "you saw the difference in the type of politician he was."

Harris went into Western Labrador to campaign for Randy Collins. His discomfort and unfamiliarity with press-the-flesh campaigning was evident through part of the day. The NDP had their office in the shopping centre, and Collins thought it would be a good idea to go out into the main corridor and do a little mainstreeting. What unfolded, confounded Callanan and Dobbin. "He just sort of stood up in the middle of the corridor," recalls Callanan. "He just stood there, and people walked by. Finally, Randy Collins said 'here's a few people, maybe we should walk up to them. He'd say "Jack Harris, NDP," as they'd walk by." Callanan wasn't sure if it was shyness on Harris' part, or if he just lacked media savvy. "Tobin would go into a mall and sweep through — 'How are you today? — How is business?' — a lot of it was plain courtesy."

The NDP have always maintained that their campaigns are about issues, not spectacle and that was made clear to Callanan one day. A few days before being assigned to the NDP campaign, Callanan had taken part in a *Here & Now* reporters' panel on impressions about the campaign so far. He recounted how Tobin was always on the move, either by helicopter or airplane, or one of the campaign's two buses. The campaign had "this fabulous sound system" and all the details appeared to have been taken care of. This kind of reporting got on Harris's nerves. He hadn't remembered it was Callanan who described this for *Here & Now*, when he complained to Callanan, "the fools, they were on the other night. Big deal, he's got two buses. He's got this sound system. And the CBC is getting caught up with that."

Harris's challenge was to expose what he felt was Tobin's and the Liberals' excess, and catapult that into an election issue. That is a fine art in politics. Only some politicians can take an event or an issue that bugs them, and make light of it without having it appear that it bugs them. Harris tried to make it an issue but he never seemed comfortable in the role. In Marystown on the last Saturday of the campaign, where he had come to support Wayne Butler against Mary Hodder, Harris had a full room of excited and enthused supporters. About Tobin's campaign, he said, "they [the Liberals] want Brian Tobin to take all the flak with his $1 million public relations campaign, his two buses and his helicopter, traveling all over the province playing hide-and-seek with reporters." Those should have been rousing words to New Democrats in Marystown, but Harris delivered it all in a monotone. The words fell flat and the expression on his face resembled that of someone who had just had his bike stolen. In this room with lots of party friends, he should have looked as if he was enjoying poking fun at Brian Tobin. But it all came out looking more like an ordeal. Substance in a campaign is what everyone should aspire to, but it would be wise for politicians to remember that people who do things well, do them effortlessly, and they look as if they are having fun.

It wasn't all bad for Harris. On the Labrador trip, he had one of the happiest moments in the whole campaign. The party was in the hunt for the seat in Western Labrador, and when he entered the airport, scores of steelworkers cheered his arrival. A similar event unfolded on the last Saturday of the campaign in Marystown.

There were no portable faxes and buses for Harris though. The NDP campaign was run on a shoestring. He drove himself in his GMC Jimmy to Marystown. The only member of his entourage was Lana Payne of the FFAW. He went alone to Western Labrador. Martin Saunders of the Canadian Labour Congress accompanied Harris to Harcourt-Burgouyne's Cove to talk to former employees of Newfoundland Slate, a company that had closed and left local people in the dark about their future prospects.

Political campaigns take place on two levels. There is the local campaign, with its local issues and the battle for a particular seat. Then there is the provincial campaign, with its focus on the leaders and the issues they define. The local campaign can run against the tide and produce an upset or two. But it is the provincial campaign that sets the tone and most times, determines who forms the government. And because of that, parties place their leaders on a platform and make the tour a tour for the media.

"You're aware of newscasts and filing times," says Dennis Brown of the Liberal tour. "It's important you determine where the filing sites are. It's no use being caught on the Northern Peninsula late in the day if you have to file a visual story. We try to organize in such a fashion that there will be pictures for the CBC News that night."

Kim Puddister of the Conservative camp says "the media is your way to get your message out and it has a large influence on the outcome of the campaign." She claims that's why the Conservatives spent the first week of the campaign close to St. John's. "It's the media centre. We had a lot less money than Brian Tobin did [to advertise]. We had to do everything to get Ed's face in the media." A point that wasn't lost on the media, was that the Conservatives had few candidates in place outside the Avalon in the first week. It would have been a public relations disaster of the worst order for Ed Byrne to be traveling to districts where the party didn't have a candidate.

The press is well aware that they are part of a program of organized events that are designed to look spontaneous and newsworthy. In the 1999 election, the Liberals and Conservatives arranged events early in the day that they felt would play best for the electronic media. Says Peter Walsh, "it [the schedule] is geared around the press. The party stuff is centred around three o'clock or later in the afternoon. Ed Byrne gave one significant speech a day and that was always done in time for the camera to record it." Since this was Walsh's first campaign, he was a little worried at the start. How would he find an interesting event or story and would he have the chance to break away from the tour to complete his story for the evening news? "I discovered they were working with me on that," he says. "They were putting the most visual and interesting stuff early in the day so I can do my job." A similar practice was followed by the Liberals. Says Callanan, "the Liberals really understood the media. They knew radio would need something for noon. TV had to file for the supper hour news. If there was a longer-style radio interview needed for the next morning, they would make room for that."

Callanan concluded the NDP wasn't near as interested in creating media events. "I'm sure the NDP would suggest their campaign was substance," he says. "They would say the Liberals were shows." The New Democrats would change their schedule for "no reason." It lacked the choreography of the Liberal campaign.

Brian Tobin readily admits campaigns are geared toward media coverage. "The press can only use two or three events, [you] find your message for the day and run those events." But he claims his campaigns are different, in that extra events are added and the entire day is occupied. Reporters agree Tobin is on the move from morning to night during the campaign. He puts it down to genetics, his "A-type personality. I couldn't stay still to save my soul." That may be so, but Tobin knows that energy translates into a dynamic feel in a campaign, and that in turn inspires candidates and party workers to keep going. In that circumstance, even if the media is unable to report on all the events, they are along for the ride and the constant motion by the leader creates the sense that this is a "happening" campaign.

In the midst of all of this "assistance" offered reporters on the campaign, how can they keep an independent view of things and report objectively? It's a dilemma the reporters on the 1999 campaign readily admit exists. Jay Callanan says "if you're on the trail, you're tied to their agenda." To get a picture of this, imagine being flown to wherever the leader is headed, landing where he lands, and being driven to the local event by party volunteers. "You're very much constrained as to where they decide to take you." Peter Walsh says "when you're out there [on the campaign], you're 100 percent at their mercy. When it comes to breaking stories, it's really tough." Reporters on the campaign have to content themselves with covering the campaign as it unfolds, reporting inconsistencies, and getting as much of the story as they can from those who come in contact with the leader. "I realized we have an entire newsroom to break stories," says Walsh, adding that treatment of the campaign through panels and issues stories can complement the coverage from the road. If not for those other treatments, the public "would get a packaged diet of events planned before two o'clock. They would get appearances and speeches in friendly environments." *The Telegram* makes extensive use of editorial boards with the leaders during elections. It prints excerpts from those interviews, and also spins off stories from those encounters.

Callanan says reporters "have to guard against getting caught up in the excitement" of a campaign. "For us," he says, "the producers will be our safeguard. They would ultimately put our feet back on the ground." Television reporters have the added benefit of a colleague — the cameraman. Says Callanan, "you bounce things off each other. If you're excited by a certain thing, the cameraman might say 'get serious.' That's how we kept the excitement to a minimum level."

Of the three campaigns, the New Democrats stand out because in recent elections, they have failed to embrace the big event road show that the Liberals have perfected, and the Conservatives have tried to emulate. All his criticism aside about road shows being all about image and not substance, Jack Harris appears to have been convinced that such shows have become necessary. He believes the public views the campaign bus and road show as evidence "that you're ready for a fight, the horse-race image of elections." Harris wants his party prepared for the next election, in order to avoid the confusion and lack of organization that characterized the lead-up to the 1999 vote. He plans to push the party to have an election plan mapped out by late 2001. "We should have mapped out a plan for the issues we expect, the themes, [the] kinds of events for the first three days of the campaign." And he feels New Democrats will have to rethink a leader's tour in the style that Liberals and Conservatives run their tours. Says Harris, the party should have a vehicle, "not necessarily a bus, [but] a large van or something where you can take media and a large number of people [on the road]." Despite his personal distaste for campaigns that go heavy on the razzle-dazzle, Harris has come to regard the trappings of a leader's tour as important in the modern Newfoundland election. He says such a tour "looks as if you have momentum. Early on, it's important to look organized."

Election Diary

Wednesday, February 3, 1999

Today is the start of a series of television interviews with the leaders of the four parties for Here & Now, our supper hour program at CBC. We're on deck early for a 9:15 interview with Brian Tobin.

Tobin is supremely confident, as always. Before the interview, he talks up the campaign. You can feel the adrenalin. A leader on a campaign that is nearly complete, is a combination of well-tuned athlete and wild-eyed caffeine-driven creature.

Tobin says the polls haven't moved since the election, "we're holding our position," he says.

The interview goes smoothly enough, except for our disagreement about employment gains in 1998. Tobin claims it's a 3.2 percent increase, higher than the Canadian average. I disagree. Statistics Canada has told me Newfoundland gained 3,000 jobs in 1998. Based on a workforce of 196,000, that's about a 1.6 percent gain. Tobin is using another kind of calculation, one that's legitimate Statistics Canada tells me, but does not accurately reflect the employment gain from one year-end to another.

Brian Tobin does not like to be contradicted. After the interview, he has his assistant Heidi Bonnell reach the province's top civil servant, Malcolm Rowe, on the cell phone. "Malcolm, Malcolm", the Premier blurts into the phone. He informs Rowe about our disagreement over the numbers, waits awhile, and finally another of his assistants, Tony Grace, tells me the Premier will call later with the numbers.

A couple of hours later, Tobin calls and tells me I'm wrong. I hold my ground, convinced of the information Statistics Canada has given me. "I'll send an Assistant Deputy Minister over right now" to show you the right numbers, Tobin tells me. I tell him that will not be necessary, that the numbers will be fine. He agrees to fax me his numbers.

I don't feel intimidated. I suppose that's the point you get to after working 17 years in an organization that supports its journalists, yet demands they get the story straight. I call Statistics Canada in Ottawa one more time and get the matter clarified. After the interview plays on tonight's show, I tell the audience both sets of employment numbers are right, "in a sense". However, Statistics Canada tells me the number I used is a more accurate representation of how the employment numbers have changed in recent months. Translation — employment is up but not by as much as the Premier claims.

The other story that gets headlines today is Tobin's reaction to the letter faxed to our newsroom yesterday by the headquarters of Paul Brown, Conservative candidate for St. John's Centre. The anonymous letter writer makes allegations that Liberal MHA Mary Hodder has received living allowances under the MHA expenses program to which she isn't entitled. Here & Now checks out the story, and the allegations prove groundless. Tobin calls for Paul Brown to pull himself out of the race and promises to hire a lawyer to pursue the case on behalf of the MHA. It sounds like a pure case of intimidation and campaign bluster, but it sets the Brown campaign back on its heels.

Shortly after 11 tonight, Brown meets with his leader Ed Byrne, who has just arrived back in town from Labrador City and Wabush. They decide Brown's campaign manager, Tim Powers, will be fired.

Chapter 12

The Road Home

The last few days before the provincial vote was a frantic time for the three leaders, as they intensified efforts to make personal appearances where it could make the biggest impact. Despite Brian Tobin's assertion that the polls had not moved since the election, the gap had narrowed considerably between the Liberals and the Conservatives. The only question was if the movement was on pace with what had happened in the 1993 and 1996 elections, when the Conservatives moved upward from their pre-election, low double-digit public approval levels only to stall at around 40 percent of the popular vote.

Inside the Conservative camp, nerves were frayed as their public approval moved upward in the late stages of the campaign. Most felt the movement in the polls had begun after the debate. While Ed Byrne had not scored a knockout, he handled himself reasonably well. The public had its first chance to see the 33-year old leader under fire. Byrne himself felt he "sawed off" the debate, a result that "was a huge victory for me," considering the public had low expectations of him in pre-debate polls.

Paul Shelley watched the debate from his Baie Verte district. He too felt the party's support increase in the few days after the debate. When support hit the 38 percent mark, Shelley was ecstatic, a few more points and the Conservatives were in the hunt for seats in the high teens or maybe even the 20's.

In the Liberal camp, veteran campaigners watched the narrowing gap with concern, but they claim, not with an overwhelming sense of alarm. Campaign chair George Furey felt the Conservatives were gaining "about the same pace" as previous elections. The Liberals weren't making big mistakes he reasoned, and he felt his champion racer, Brian Tobin, would bring the election home with a strong majority.

The New Democrats had their own drama unfolding. The leader, Jack Harris was in a close fight to hold on to his seat in Signal Hill-Quidi Vidi in the east end of St. John's. Randy Collins was in tight against a resurgent Liberal Perry Canning in Labrador West. And in a third seat, shipyard union leader Wayne Butler was gaining support against Liberal Mary Hodder in Burin-Placentia West. The New Democrats had no design on the government, but two seats would double their presence in the House. Three seats would be seen as a major victory and a base for the party to grow.

There was one factor more than any other that cast its long shadow over the entire campaign in the last week, and that was the first ministers' meeting on healthcare in Ottawa. Once it became clear early in the week that the meeting would take place, the anticipation of what it would produce in terms of extra money for healthcare, began to dominate the political debate. The political opposition found itself incapable of making headway on the issue once the meeting was announced. Brian Tobin capitalized on the meeting, first by alluding to the potential extra money and what that would do to help the healthcare system, and then later, by announcing there would be more funding.

Tobin returned to the province from Ottawa on Thursday evening, giving a scrum to reporters at the Gander Hotel before leaving in his bus with Gander MHA Sandra Kelly, Exploits MHA Roger Grimes, Fortune Bay-Cape La Hune MHA Oliver Langdon, Twillingate-Fogo MHA Gerry Reid and Melvin Penney from Lewisporte for a rally in the town of Lewisporte. Tobin told reporters attending the scrum in Gander "everything the Government of Canada transfers" for healthcare would be used in healthcare. Ryan Cleary of *The Telegram* wanted to know if this extra money would be used toward pay increases for nurses.

Cleary: Can nurses expect any more than 7 percent over three years, any more than has already been given to other public servants?

Tobin: Now, have you been designated chief negotiating agent on behalf of the nurses' union?

Cleary: No, can they expect any more? That's what they want to know.

Tobin: I'm not going to negotiate with nurses. It has to be done at the collective bargaining table.

Conservative Paul Shelley began to smell political trouble for the Conservatives. Like most Conservatives, Shelley saw the Ottawa trip as an unwelcome development in the campaign. "Unprecedented" is how he described Tobin's decision to leave the province for the meeting, and a "maneuvering and manipulative move." The Conservatives' upward movement in their opinion polls stalled. Said Shelley, "once he gave a bit of security to the fact that healthcare would be secured, our polls leveled out." Shelley figures Tobin and the Liberals were 5 or 6 days from losing the government when the healthcare funding issue appeared to be resolved, although that is not a view all Conservatives share. Still, in his own district of Baie Verte, Tobin's Ottawa trip had an effect. Shelley said even some of his own supporters remarked, "at least boy, they're going to put some money back into healthcare."

Ed Byrne regards the Tobin trip to Ottawa as "the sham of the election," but he admits it achieved Tobin's objective of showing he had obtained a solution for healthcare. Says Byrne, "on Bill Rowe's open line, he says I'm just back from the first ministers' meeting on healthcare, we have millions for healthcare." And in true Tobin fashion says Byrne, the Premier casts all the good news in a kind of mystery. "He can't say how much money it is," says Byrne, "that it's not his place." The effect though for the Conservatives was quick and it ended any hope of finishing in the high teen's or low 20's in seats. "It softens the blow for nurses, it softens the blow on patients," says the Conservative leader. "It's the number one issue and he stopped the bleed. Brian Tobin put the tourniquet on what would have been an artery." Byrne saw the whole act as a sham because once the federal budget came down, Newfoundland began to complain it wasn't getting any of the extra healthcare money. Paul Dicks and

Brian Tobin were highly critical of Ottawa. Ottawa had increased healthcare funding by billions of dollars, but the purpose of that was to restore funding to Ontario, Alberta and British Columbia. Those three provinces lost heavily when Ottawa reduced per capita healthcare funding to those provinces in the early 1990's.

Cabinet ministers like Kevin Aylward reject the suggestion of a sham on Tobin's part. Aylward says the commitment Tobin felt he had from the meeting in Ottawa was real. He says Tobin concluded he had more healthcare money "because he had met with the Prime Minister and the other premiers" and because of the interpretations of those discussions. At the end of it all, Newfoundland did get more money, but it came through an increase in equalization funding, not the program that directly funds healthcare. And much of that extra funding was intended to be a 'one-time' transfer to provinces like Newfoundland, so the funding issue has not been solved yet.

Whatever the subsequent interpretation of the Ottawa meeting, and notwithstanding the unhappiness at this turn of events in the Conservatives camp, Tobin had an issue that he now planned to present as a solution. His answers to all the questions and protests about healthcare would be framed from the perspective that he now had a solution.

In Clarenville the day after his return from Ottawa, Tobin was confronted by criticism from nurses that he had helped create the crisis in healthcare by his participation in federal budget cuts as a cabinet minister in Jean Chretien's government. "He took the money in the first place," blared a headline in *The Telegram*. The paper reported, "despite the release of new healthcare money, Tobin faces criticism for having helped take it away."

But Brian Tobin didn't much care about the criticism. His strategy would now be to turn the tables on his critics and to cast himself in the role as statesman, while his opponents were acting more like political bottom feeders. "Look, everybody who cares about healthcare, instead of looking for political advantage, should celebrate what happened yesterday." And as if to reinforce that he had made the case for more funding directly to the Prime Minister and that he had been heard, Tobin repeated for reporters what he claimed the Prime Minister said as they came out of the meeting at 24 Sussex Drive. "His words were that he had heard about the stress and strain in the healthcare system on the nurses of Newfoundland and Labrador during the meeting. I passed on what I've been hearing."

Tobin was now able to respond more specifically to concerns nurses had raised at practically every stop he made during the campaign. "I've been convinced that the [staffing] issue needs to be addressed and it's one that I intend to intervene in personally," he said. "You can't have stressed-out people working double shifts, being called back on short notice, burned-out, running and operating within the system." In Clarenville with three days left in the campaign, he told nurses demonstrating outside the G.B Cross Hospital "I think we'll be able to address some of the issues you've been talking about."

One senior Liberal argues the Ottawa trip didn't "rescue" the election for the party, rather "the stuff he [Tobin] did with the nurses was far more beneficial to us." He says Tobin's decision to talk to the nurses and empathize with their plight "certainly created the impression that some good was going to befall the nurses. It certainly took the pressure off."

Tobin himself downplays the importance of the Ottawa meeting in the latter stages of the campaign. He is only willing to concede the meeting was "helpful" in that "it reminded people the issue was bigger than Newfoundland and Labrador." Tobin argues the meeting was unhelpful "to the extent it focused on healthcare." He says commentators and losing politicians "tend to want to dissect election campaigns" and come up with "what if" scenarios. Tobin says his own equivalent "what if" is "what if we [didn't have] the schools and nurses issue."

With just five days left before the vote, Jack Harris continued on with his campaign on the west coast, just having returned from Western Labrador where Randy Collins was in a race with Perry Canning. Harris went to the hospital in Corner Brook with his candidates for Humber East and West, did a quick tour through McDonald's, appeared on Bill Rowe's Open Line show, and had breakfast with candidates and supporters. The breakfast meeting took place at the Holiday Inn in Corner Brook, and was the low-key type of event that dominated the NDP campaign. "Mr. Tobin seems to be very busy putting on a good show," Harris told the assembled group, repeating a theme he used frequently in the campaign. He talked with supporters about seniors and children living in poverty and how "it's not regarded as a crisis by the government."

One of the breakfast guests complained how the neighbouring Bay of Islands district had been represented by Premiers in the last three elections [Clyde Wells in two elections and Brian Tobin from 1996-1999], and still there was "nothing done." Harris's reply that "they must feel taken for granted," brought a response that summed up his party's chances on the West Coast. Said one man at the breakfast, "And people will vote for them [the Liberals] anyway."

Chapter 13

Final Week

The last week of an election campaign is a time of happiness and relief for candidates, the leaders, the press, and likely the public. Campaign managers warn candidates and leaders about the dangers of coasting to a finish. This is the one part of the campaign where complacency can ruin the chance to win. And even in an election that was not considered close, the Liberals and Conservatives knew the gap between them had narrowed considerably since the election call, and a fumble or sign of weakness in the last week could turn an easy win into a close victory or even minority government.

Many of the veterans around the Liberal campaign had adopted the "take a pill" approach to the final week. There was no need to panic. Yes, the lead in the polls would narrow, but the key was the Liberal vote itself. Said one insider, "it's important that your numbers are staying solid. Our numbers were always solid." The Liberal vote stayed in the high 40's to low 50's in all their polls, proof that even if the other parties were gaining, the government's support was high enough to guarantee the election.

The second place party in an election will often resort to releasing the "results" of a poll late in the campaign in order to show the public that the race is closer than the pundits and the leading party suggest. There are many cases in Newfoundland politics, and probably politics in other places, where parties have released contrived polls or contrived results.

In 1999, the Conservatives had a $10,000 poll carried out in the last week of the election by a polling firm from Toronto. Ed Byrne badly wanted to have the results published. Byrne claims he talked to both the CBC and NTV and asked "if we did a poll, would you release it?" Byrne claims both agreed to run the polls with certain conditions attached. He says the poll results "showed us within 7 points," but both CBC and NTV refused to carry the results. He claims CBC Radio in Newfoundland got closest to running the poll results on the Saturday morning before the election, "but it got stopped by CBC national [national news managers in Toronto]." Byrne called the episode "unfortunate" and claimed the poll "was a story, it was the truth."

Both CBC and NTV were skeptical of the poll because the Conservatives refused to provide details about the polling company and how they carried out the survey. CBC has a further requirement where reporters have to be able to get access to representatives of the polling firm in order to ask questions. When none of those conditions were met, CBC refused to carry the results. Veteran *Here & Now* producer John Furlong dealt with the Conservatives on the poll. He claims there was no deal, and when the Conservatives refused to provide information about the company that carried out the polling and how to reach them, *Here & Now* decided it would not consider carrying the results of the poll.

Incidentally, John's brother, Jim Furlong, is news director at NTV. He says NTV didn't undertake to run results of the poll. Jim Furlong says they did have a "major debate" in the NTV newsroom about using the poll results. He says the decision came down to whether releasing the poll results would be seen as a partisan broadcast, since the Conservatives had paid for the poll. "Would it be seen as an ad?" NTV, like CBC, decided it would not run a story on the poll.

The final week though, was more than a debate over polling. Healthcare had kept up a steady temperature through the campaign, and the demonstrations by nurses continued to dog Tobin and his cabinet ministers. In location after location, Tobin agreed that healthcare was an important issue and he would do his best to fix the system. Ironically, it was this issue that had caused so him much grief, that would provide him the opportunity to be seen as a champion for healthcare.

A first ministers meeting had been planned for Ottawa for Thursday, February 4, just five days before election day. Politicians don't like to be out of the province during an election, but Tobin and his advisers allowed this was not a meeting that could be missed. The Prime Minister and Finance Minister had already suggested there would be more money made available for the Canadian healthcare system, and this meeting would put a stamp on this general direction just in time for the federal budget in late February. For Tobin, the timing was perfect.

Jean Chretien likes Brian Tobin, but didn't appreciate the very public posturing the Newfoundland Premier had been engaged in for months previous. Tobin had traveled the country, partly on public business, but also it was believed, in an apparent attempt to persuade Liberals that he would be a potential leadership candidate once Chretien retired. Still, when Chretien looks at Canada's political map, most of the friendly Liberal faces have disappeared. By the fall of 1999, Brian Tobin was the only Liberal premier left.

If Tobin were to attend the First Ministers Meeting, he would need to get there fast. That was no problem, according to the Prime Minister. He would send a Challenger jet to pick up the Premier, and have him back to Newfoundland by the next evening to resume his campaigning.

Tobin now saw opportunity on the healthcare issue. About leaving the campaign, he told reporters — "the dividends may be worth it: a possible healthcare accord and more money for the province's healthcare system." Reported *The Telegram*, "he pledged Tuesday at a number of campaign stops to invest every new dollar from Ottawa for healthcare, in healthcare." Tobin could never be accused of understating things, especially if there is a way to enhance his own position. Even as he knew there would be more money for healthcare, he told reporters and campaign audiences about the need to "wrestle" the money from Ottawa. The translated message — 'it might not be an easy job, but I am the one leader who can do it.'

The last week of the campaign is a time when candidates in losing fights have to drag out all the rhetoric they've assembled in their years in politics, and see if it works one more time with the public. In Lewisporte, where nearly everyone felt Liberal Melvin Penney was in trouble, he made a last gasp for a chance to hang on as the MHA.

"The doom and gloom is now optimism," Penney told the local paper, *The Pilot*. "The support I received was overwhelming." Penney regarded his having survived the nomination challenge from three other Liberals as a clear sign of the party's strength in the district. "To have four Liberals running in a district where the PC's couldn't find one single solitary candidate out of 8,000 voters and had to bring someone from outside the district — it just shows the level of support that's here."

Brian Tobin himself attempted to put a lift into two badly faltering Liberal campaigns. Barbara Howlett was up against Conservative leader Ed Byrne in Kilbride, and Harold Mullowney had taken on former leader, and now high profile opposition health critic Loyola Sullivan in Ferryland. On a swing through both districts on the last weekend of the campaign, Tobin turned up the rhetoric. In Kilbride, many of Barbara Howlett's campaign workers came outside the headquarters to greet Tobin as he got off the bus. Then, putting an arm around Howlett, and in range of the cameras and the microphones, Tobin began his performance. "My wife was here knocking on doors last week — I was in central Newfoundland," he told Howlett. "She called me and said 'Brian, there's something happening in Kilbride. You've got to get out here with Barbara because there's a victory to be had'." Howlett, who must by now have sensed that the Liberal wind in Kilbride was blowing at less than gale force, replied "oh yes, yes indeed it is."

And in Ferryland, where the Liberals managed to put together a large motorcade, Tobin boasted the Ferryland district would become Liberal red this time. It was enough to spook some Conservatives. Loyola Sullivan himself called Bill Rowe's Open Line and said "we'll see who's lying on election day."

Tobin's foray into Kilbride and Ferryland is part of a tactic that had two purposes. The first was to show some support to Liberal candidates who were up against formidable competition. After all, Ed Byrne and Loyola Sullivan are the two highest profile politicians in the Conservative party. The second reason is somewhat more strategic. In the dying days of the campaign, parties will put on the push in close districts, something that's true for the opposition as well as the government. Loyola Sullivan, feeling comfortable in Ferryland, might want to help out in adjacent districts. Ed Byrne would want to be on the road in a few of the close districts, hoping his presence would steer a few more votes to the Conservatives. By stamping on their turf, and boasting about it, and organizing a large motorcade, the Liberals were attempting to inject a little uncertainty into Ferryland and Kilbride. The added bonus might be that such a display would keep Byrne and Sullivan at home, rather than out on the road helping other Conservatives.

Election Diary

Thursday, February 4, 1999

We had studio interviews today with Sue Kelland-Dyer of the Newfoundland and Labrador Party and Ed Byrne. Both interviews have gone well. Byrne has looked better as the campaign progresses. He was strong tonight, answering questions directly, including ones about the Brown letter and Pilar Riego.

Byrne claims the polls are moving in his direction. He tells me the Conservatives will hold on to the 10 seats they have, and that they are within 4 to 5 points in 17 other seats. He will focus his efforts on close seats in the days from now until the election.

Before her interview, Sue Kelland-Dyer admits she toyed with running for the Conservatives "for 10 minutes", confirming a rumour we had heard. Dyer says the other parties are always asking her about running for them, but she decided to stay with the cause. Two of the party's former executives are running for other parties — Paul Hunt for the Conservatives and Dan Corbett for the New Democrats.

Kelland-Dyer, as usual is well-prepared and easily speaks to the issues. I sense from her expression she does not appreciate having been confronted with the idea of running for another party.

Chapter 14

Sue and Ed

Sue Kelland-Dyer and her party, the Newfoundland and Labrador Party had gone through a prolonged rough spot in the year prior to the election. First, the party's high-profile founding member Al Chislett, removed himself from the group. In the weeks and months after this, the party was enveloped by confusion as members questioned Sue Kelland-Dyer's legitimacy as interim leader. Kelland-Dyer herself questioned the commitment of a group on the executive who she felt worked at cross-purposes with the party's goal of creating awareness about resource policy. The party believed properly developed and implemented resource policy would set Newfoundland on the road to a new era of prosperity that had so far eluded Canada's youngest province.

But politics is also about practical things. Heading into the election, the Conservatives were anxious to put as many "star" candidates as possible on the ballot, and Sue Kelland-Dyer was considered a star.

Most people in Newfoundland know Kelland-Dyer as an outspoken advocate of Newfoundland through radio open-line shows. Kelland-Dyer started out as a Liberal, but tore up her party membership in the early 1990's as then-Liberal Premier Clyde Wells contemplated selling Newfoundland and Labrador Hydro. For Kelland-Dyer, such an act was tantamount to treason. Newfoundland was poor she maintained, because of previous resource giveaways. Churchill Falls, the fishery, Labrador iron ore were all given as examples.

The Conservatives opposed privatization and considered Kelland-Dyer and her fellow open-line callers as soulmates. She was hired by then-leader Len Simms to work in his office. But the

Conservatives were shocked to find that Kelland-Dyer was still calling open-line radio shows voicing her concerns. After all, it's the politicians who get to make public statements on behalf of the party. The Conservatives were unwilling to continue having Kelland-Dyer in that role, and she was unwilling to tolerate being stifled, so they parted company.

So it was the practical side of politics that brought the two sides together in a hotel room at the Traveller's Inn in St. John's in the early days of the 1999 election. Ed Byrne met with Kelland-Dyer four times in the first three days of election, hoping to entice her to run for the Conservatives. Byrne maintains she was "seriously considering running for us". One of the meetings was attended by Dave Johnson, President of the Newfoundland and Labrador Party. Byrne and Johnson knew each other from their involvement in the labour movement years before. Said Byrne, "we sat down and went through our policies. Sue could have run for us and won a seat." The Conservatives felt a lot was riding on those talks. One senior official says Kelland-Dyer's candidacy for the Conservatives would have virtually killed the Newfoundland and Labrador Party, and created some momentum for the Conservatives.

Byrne himself had to cross a tough mental bridge before he consented to seriously consider having Kelland-Dyer as a running mate. After all, she had quit two parties, including the Conservatives, after having serious disagreements. Yet, Byrne was taken with the prospect of having someone of Kelland-Dyer's profile as a candidate. He made up his mind after talking with Walter Manning, a lifelong Conservative and successful businessman from St. Bride's. Walter Manning is the father of Fabian Manning, the one-term member for St. Mary's-The Capes, and in the 1999 election, attempting to make a comeback as the Conservative candidate in the district of Placentia-St. Mary's. Byrne respected Walter Manning's opinion and his political instinct. "Ed, this is an election," the elder Manning told the young Conservative leader, "You have to win seats. She can win a seat."

Sue Kelland-Dyer would only admit toying with the offer. As it was, she said no to the Conservatives and ran in the district of

Conception Bay East-Bell Island for the Newfoundland and Labrador Party. The party would field seven candidates in the election and take close to 2 percent of the popular vote.

Friday, February 5, 1999

Jack Harris is not your rah-rah type of politician. He is not a spin doctor. He is matter-of-fact in his pronouncements. That gives Harris a "common" touch, but in an election where Brian Tobin dominates media coverage with an opposite image, it may amount to a large liability for Harris.

I believe I finally figured out today why Harris has not been the breakthrough force New Democrats hoped when they elected him leader in 1992. He does not take the "first among equals" role that leaders generally do. There is no campaign entourage catering to his every need; he's not boasting about the large crowds he has been able to attract. Of course, that is not easy to do when you are a caucus of one.

Harris was the last of the leaders to come to our studio for an interview. The performance was steady, and he probably scored a few points with his insistence that Brian Tobin must take more blame for the state of the healthcare system. After all, he argues, Tobin was an influential minister in Ottawa when the first cuts were made.

The Liberals are no strangers to spin, but even in this campaign, there are some nuggets of truth emerging. Brian Tobin will not go into Western Labrador to campaign with Liberal MHA Perry Canning. A source in the Liberal party confirms Tobin's presence could provoke more anger at the candidate. "Perry wants to do this in his own way," I'm told.

The Conservatives are planning to blitz several districts over the remaining few days. They will keep the districts close to their chest until their polling reveals where to go. Ed Byrne will visit the close ones, hoping to tweak up the support a few more points.

The Conservatives want to win the government, but they are realistic. Any gains on their part will be a blow to Tobin. This will not be the Frank McKenna-type washout some Liberals predicted. Byrne has not been caught offside; he has been caught in a sea of doubt about his ability to win the elec-

tion. That seriously impaired the early recruitment of candidates the party so desperately wanted. Byrne will not admit this, but filling candidates spots in the once-Conservative stronghold of Burin Peninsula on the last day before close of nominations, is not a good sign.

In Fortune Bay-Cape La Hune, the Conservative spot was filled at virtually the last minute when Bob Baker filed nomination papers. Baker had indicated his interest in running for the party when Byrne was in Corner Brook early in the campaign. With the nomination deadline approaching, and Fortune Bay-Cape La Hune having no candidate, Byrne called Baker and asked him to take on Oliver Langdon. That led to a dramatic last-minute scurry for the party. Baker was in St. John's and faxed his papers to the returning office in the district. But you can't fax money. So the Conservatives had to hurry and get one of their supporters in the district to rush up to the returning officer's house with $100 to cover Baker's nomination fee.

Chapter 15

Polling Day

Polling day is the naked moment of truth in politics. It is the time when there is no longer any benefit to boasting, nothing to gain by inflating poll numbers, and it is futile to posture. The time for pretense is over. Candidates who have endured tough, and perhaps losing campaigns, have to face what they know in their heart and soul. Those who feel comfortable cannot show themselves to be too smug, since their fate is not in their own hands, but in the hands of the voters. It is the time of truth.

The tension and nerves were almost palpable in Labrador West. Randy Collins got up early, wondering how he would spend the next fourteen hours until the polls closed. If everything went as the NDP campaign felt it would, tonight they would have a victory party. But Collins wasn't willing to put money down on that prospect. The votes weren't in the ballot box yet.

In the early morning, the phone rang at his house several times, friends from his hometown of Gambo, from Ontario and western Canada wishing him good luck. Finally, the polls opened, and he and his wife went out to vote. But what to do for the rest of the day?

He made his way down to headquarters where there was a continuous chatter as campaign workers phoned party supporters, reminding them this was the big day. Collins learned on polling day the candidate is not of much use to the cause. "I went up [to the headquarters] a few times and was basically told I was in the way." Collins returned to his house and pondered driving down to his cabin on Ashuanipi Lake, not far away from Perry Canning's cabin. He decided to stay home and began to read. "I did a bit of reading to try to get my mind off it a bit," he says, "but basically I suffered a long day." Once six o'clock came, he sat down and watched the television news. The long wait was pretty well over.

Across town, Perry Canning's hope had turned to resignation. The late surge in the campaign as a large block of the undecided turned his way, was not enough to stem the tide. Unless there was a miracle, his time as an MHA was over. He had felt lonely many times in the previous six months as people in western Labrador vented their anger at him and the government over the pellet plant issue. But he had never felt as alone as when the light faded from the Labrador City sky on polling day.

As Randy Collins sat down to watch the television news, Perry Canning got in his van and drove down Hudson Drive, Labrador City's main street. He turned into the parking lot next to the Roman Catholic church, knocked on the door of the residence, and went inside. Unable to understand, maybe unable to accept what was unfolding, he sat and talked with the Roman Catholic Bishop. Perry Canning is not a Roman Catholic, but he had grown to know and respect the Bishop. "I said 'Bishop Doug, I will lose by 200 votes,' he recalls. Filled with hurt, he told the Bishop how difficult a time he had accepting that "people somehow thought I wasn't telling the truth, that I wasn't being forthright, that I was covering up for the government." He spent a half hour unburdening his soul to the Bishop, then left and returned home.

Canning gathered his wife and two children in the living room and told them what he had told the bishop. "We talked about it and I told them it was my view we would lose," he recalls. "We should prepare for that. We should stick it out as a family and be graceful."

Harbour Main-Whitbourne had been conceded privately by Liberals to the Conservative Tom Hedderson. Hedderson knew this but didn't want to let on to his workers. "I got up in the morning and took the view I was 1000 votes behind," he says. His fear was that complacency could wreck his campaign, and steal a victory.

Harbour Main-Whitbourne has three main population centres — the Harbour Main-Avondale area, Whitbourne, and the Brigus area. For both practical and political reasons, Hedderson had three headquarters. He had already made up his mind before election day that he wouldn't choose one headquarters over another to wait out the election results. Hedderson decided to stay at his mother-in-law's house in Harbour Main. Surrounded by his wife, children, and brothers and sisters who came from St. John's, they waited to see if the man who joined the Conservatives in the John Crosbie movement of 1971, would now take a seat with his adopted party in the legislature.

St. John's Centre was a close race. The Liberals knew it. The Conservatives knew it. The Liberal camp had it all on the line. Their health minister, Joan Marie Aylward, was involved in one of the tightest races in the entire province, with healthcare having emerged as the most important issue. Her campaign had furiously beaten back a plan by party headquarters during the campaign to send Aylward to a health ministers' meeting on the social union in British Columbia. She simply could not afford two travel days and one meeting day in such a close campaign.

Election day dawned sunny and cool in St. John's. Aylward's campaign leaped into action and blanketed the seniors' complexes in the district. By quarter to eleven, only two of the residents at Rickett's Manor in the downtown had not voted, "and they would vote at noon." Throughout the day, workers who had fanned out to private homes in the district, phoned the voters on their lists who had been identified in door-to-door canvassing as Liberal supporters. As people came to the polling stations, their names were crossed off the list. By 5:30, campaign manager Ted Lomond was getting concerned. Several hundred people on their list of identified voters still had not gone to the polls. To do nothing would be the same as surrendering the seat. Workers who had been phoning all day were now instructed to get in their cars and go door-to-door and state their case for Joan Marie Aylward. Says Lomond, "we'd say Mrs. Smith, I noticed you hadn't voted. It's a close election. Joan Marie really needs your support. Can you come with us now and we'll take you to the polling station?" "Hundreds" of people were coaxed out to the polls says Lomond. It did not come without a battle though, he claims. Some workers were uncomfortable with going door-to-door and having to practically drag people out of their warm homes into the cold night air. He asked some of the campaign's more forward workers to go to the doors and do the job.

At eight o'clock, a crowd started gathering to watch the evening unfold on the big board in the main room of Aylward's headquarters. Lomond brought Aylward in through the back fire exit to see the results as they came in over his phone line. Aylward would see the results first and have the chance to prepare herself for victory or defeat, away from the supporters in the next room.

Yvonne Jones returned home early on election morning from Cartwright, a one hour plane ride. She talked to friends, many people stopped by her house for tea. But there was nervous energy even in this district, where Liberals have always polled well. "There are always butterflies," she says. "You can never be sure how people will vote." Jones kept herself busy. She baked a cake and took it over to James Rumbolt, the oldest man in Mary's Harbour, whose 90th birthday fell on election day. Then Jones took a walk in the cold, crisp air.

Chapter 16

Conclusion

Politics has often been defined as the competition for scarce resources. That is certainly part of it, but only part. Politics is also the interpretation of public events, and when it comes to the outcome of elections, how people see them depends on where they sit, and more precisely, which party they back.

The indisputable conclusion from the 1999 provincial general election is that the Liberals won a majority government, they lost seats, and some of their popular vote was eroded. When you move beyond those basic facts though, there is room for all kinds of discussion about who had momentum in the late stages of the campaign, what these results could mean for the next election, and how the outcome might affect the political future of Brian Tobin, Ed Byrne and Jack Harris.

Whether it was overconfidence, cockiness, or just plain boastfulness, some Liberals headed into the election believing they would wipe Ed Byrne and the Conservatives practically off the political map. Said one Liberal cabinet minister, "I had no doubt he [Tobin] would win the election. I thought we would be closer to 40 [seats] depending on the roll the campaign would get on." Another recalled some Liberals felt they would sweep the Conservatives. "I never thought we would win that [big]. Brian would say 'how many seats will we win?' He wanted to hear 45. I thought we would lose a few. Oh no, no!" would be the reply.

Finance minister Paul Dicks has been involved in Liberal elections both as a candidate and party official since the early 1980's. His theory is that the opinion polls going into elections give only an indication of how things will turn out. "Clyde Wells thought we would win 52 seats in 1993, his approval rating was over 50 percent. Len

Simms was 9 percent." Yet, says Dicks, the Conservatives came out of that election with about 40 percent of the vote. Dicks' theory, which some others share, is that there is such a thing in recent Newfoundland elections as "bedrock" support. Simply put, no matter how poorly a party appears to be doing in opinion polls prior to an election, it will poll a certain predictable percentage of the vote. Since the Conservatives lost the government in 1989, their support has hovered around 40 percent. Dicks feels the key for winning the government in that kind of electoral environment is for a party to acquire "the swing vote," the 15 or 20 percent of votes that could be up for grabs during the election.

The 1999 election saw the Liberals returned to power with 32 seats, four fewer than they held in the previous Assembly; the Conservatives with 14 seats, four more than before the election; and the NDP gained a seat and now has two members.

From the Liberal side, the first goal was to get back into government. They achieved that, but their performance was not as good as they had hoped. Forestry and Agriculture Minister Kevin Aylward, who won his Stephenville East seat, tries to be philosophical. "In this business, if you shoot for 38 or 40, and get 30-odd, that's quite satisfactory." He acknowledges though, that voters took out their anger on the Liberals during the campaign. "At the end of the day, even when people were frustrated, that's what won him a second mandate [Tobin's promise to negotiate good deals on Churchill Falls and Voisey's Bay]." Campaign manager George Furey rejects any concern over losing seats. "We're quite happy with it [the result]," he says. "Any time you can run on your record and maintain the government, you're happy." Tobin himself points to the nearly 50 recent of the vote achieved by the Liberals in 1999 as evidence of a satisfactory finish. Demonstrations by nurses and the school board report on the Avalon took the focus from his campaign, he says. "Against that backdrop, I was very happy [with the result]."

The Conservatives were vulnerable heading into the election. They had a new leader, their war chest was empty, and the prevailing sense that the party was out of the race before it started, did little to bring potential candidates off the sidelines and into the race. Some members lamented privately how they wished their leader had some of the charisma and vitality that Brian Tobin possessed.

Yet, opposition political parties and their leaders know the sad fact of political life is that they have to run in elections, and pretend everything is okay, even if things are very much awry. In the 1999 election, the Conservatives had to wade through money problems, tackle the problems finding candidates, and they had to overcome doubts about their leader.

Paul Shelley ran a comfortable campaign in Baie Verte. Neither Shelley, nor any of the other nine Conservative incumbents had a problem retaining their seats. He views the election outcome as much closer than Liberals, and even the commentators, have suggested. When you put the election in perspective he says, "we went from a party with a new leader, a snap election in mid-winter," and turned it into "41 percent of the popular vote, 14 members, we missed getting five cabinet ministers by 2000 votes (Joan Marie Aylward, Kevin Aylward, Sandra Kelly, Roger Grimes, and Ernie McLean). If we had turned over 5 percent of the vote, we could have had a majority government."

Similarly, and perhaps predictably for an opposition leader, given that the job is always on the line, Ed Byrne feels a few twists and turns toward his party could have meant a different result. "I thought we could have won 20 seats, 18 or 20 seats." Byrne felt there was some momentum toward the Conservatives as the campaign progressed, and that, combined with the undecided vote, could have propelled his party toward government. "The undecided can move," he points out, "if you get to the point where you are in the hunt, anything can happen with a week left."

But something else bears examination. Elections are run by people and they are headed by leaders. And by anyone's account, Brian Tobin was felt to be experienced enough to carry the day. Brian Tobin knows how to win elections, and perhaps more important in the winter of 1999, his challenge was to prevent dissatisfaction with the government from spoiling his return to power. People close to Tobin said he did it through a variety of means. For one thing, he believes strongly in keeping morale high. Each time he returned to

St. John's, Tobin visited party headquarters and said hello to the staff who worked there. He would deliver a short speech to thank everyone for their contribution. As one campaign staffer said, he looked relaxed, "as if he had just come back from two weeks vacation." Such a performance by the leader reinvigorates campaign staff who themselves, may be tired or cranky.

On the campaign trail, Brian Tobin did at least two major things to confront the dissatisfaction that developed over healthcare and other issues. He generally engaged protesters in discussion, promising to promise nothing at the moment, but agreeing to look at solutions other than money (as he did with nurses). And he took the dissatisfaction seriously enough that new Liberal ads were developed on healthcare, proof that a campaign, even one that starts with a particular theme (leadership), has to change to reflect the new concerns or be in danger of collapsing.

The backdrop to the campaign was the mystery about Brian Tobin's motive in calling the election less than three years after his previous mandate. Much of the discussion had to do with his perceived Prime Ministerial ambitions, little of it focused on thorny domestic issues such as the threat of a nurses' strike. Yet, sources inside the government claim he was concerned enough about a strike by nurses, to consider a couple of potential windows for an election before a strike could happen.

Tobin himself made an effort in an interview with *Here & Now* to dispel the notion that he wanted this election out of the way in order to be ready if the Prime Minister decided to not run in the next federal election. I wanted to know if he would stay for his full term if he was reelected.

> Letto: I want to ask you this question straight on — and that is —will you stay on for a full 4-year term?
>
> Tobin: Yes, I will.
>
> Letto: The entire 4 years?
>
> Tobin: Yes, I will.
>
> Letto: You're not going anywhere in the next few months?

Tobin: No, I'm not.

At the time, some Liberals felt Tobin had no choice but to state firmly he was staying. Anything less than that would have made him the issue, and his motive in going through the expense of an early election, all the more called into question. It was easier to deal with the issue this way, than it was to appear to leave the door open just a little and invite questions and press coverage about his ambitions when his primary job was to return the Liberals to power.

With the election a distant memory in the fall of 1999, many Liberals felt Tobin's declaration that he would stay in Newfoundland for a full term, was a necessary requirement in order to keep everyone's focus on the campaign. Now, any number of them sketch out scenarios under which he might be enticed to go into the battle of his life — a contest for the leadership of the Liberal Party of Canada.

Liberals in Newfoundland generally see three competitors for the Liberal leadership if Jean Chretien leaves — Finance Minister Paul Martin, Health Minister Allan Rock, and Brian Tobin. Tobin is regarded as a red Liberal, stronger on social issues than Martin, and more able to launch an emotional appeal to Liberals. Martin on the other hand, is more fiscally conservative, and more likely to preach a stay-the-course strategy. Alan Rock may be positioned in such a run-off to be a dark horse, and could sweep up the middle and claim the leadership.

The people who watch this scenario closely in Newfoundland Liberal circles, and there are many of them, since Tobin's departure would lead to a provincial leadership convention, point to factors that give Martin and Rock an advantage over the Newfoundland Premier. Both can boast continuous service in Ottawa, while Tobin has been away from the capital for several years. One Newfoundland Liberal insider feels Martin and Rock have likely used the intervening time to further their own interests with Liberal backbenchers, "doing little favours here [and there] for somebody...when the time comes, who are those MP's going to support?" This kind of activity he says, would make it difficult for Tobin to build key federal caucus support for a leadership run.

Other Liberals feel that Tobin's profile will only be enhanced, now that he's the only remaining Liberal premier in the country. And there is also the feeling that Brian Tobin's youth and his vast network across the country could serve him well if he wants to run for the Liberal leadership.

Conservatives feel Brian Tobin has run his last campaign as Liberal leader in Newfoundland. Paul Shelley says Newfoundland isn't a big enough media centre for Tobin, who "likes walking the corridors of Parliament Hill and being on the national media." Conservative campaign manager Loyola Hearn believes Tobin's chances for national leadership improve if Jean Chretien stays on for another term. If Chretien leaves he says, Paul Martin is so far ahead "it doesn't matter who wins."

Brian Tobin has never announced his interest in the national leadership, but he has hinted in several ways that it would hold some appeal. So far in his political career, Tobin has won most of his political fights. His friends and political confidantes claim he is careful and calculating in the political risks he takes, and none of them expect him to jump into a national leadership race without being sure he is in the game. And if he feels it is not worth the risk, Brian Tobin will likely say he was never interested in the job anyway.

Ed Byrne attempts to excuse himself from the discussion about his political future as leader of the Conservatives. "I'm the wrong person to ask," he says in response to a question about whether he will lead the party in the next election. Byrne does want the party to know he'd like to stay, and that he is committed to the Conservatives. "I am in this for the long haul," he states, "it is my plan to take the party into the next election."

Byrne gives a clue as to how he would put his case if he were challenged for the party leadership. "I think I'm in a stronger position than I was 14 or 15 months ago," he claims, referring to his having taken over a party with 10 seats and faring poorly in the polls, and then leading the Conservatives to 14 seats. "Has it [the election result] positioned me better?" he asks rhetorically, certain that there is just one conceivable answer. "Probably."

Ed Byrne is where many opposition leaders have been before, both in his own party, and in the now-governing Liberals. The challenge becomes — how does he take his party from its modest improvement in the 1999 election through the next three or four years, and place himself in position to contend for power next time. Holding on to the reins of power in opposition is always more difficult than it seems. Ask Leo Barry.

Barry was the highly-regarded energy minister in Brian Peckford's first cabinet. He didn't see eye-to-eye with Peckford and left to cross the floor to the Liberals. Barry eventually became leader and led the party to a 7-seat improvement in the 1985 election. Many Liberals, and even Conservatives conceded, that had the election lasted a few more days, Barry might have made the conversion from Conservative energy minister to Liberal premier in less than three years. But he did not get the chance.

While Barry was out of the country in the spring of 1986, the Liberal caucus planned a revolt. He returned to face his accusers. Placing second in the 1985 election seemed an accomplishment at the time, but it was not enough for a party that had now developed the "opposition complex" — when the party fails, blame it on the leader. Barry had learned the lesson, but so had his predecessors in the post-Smallwood era. Roberts, Jamieson, and Stirling had lost elections as opposition leaders. To live the life of an opposition leader who has lost one election is to walk on dangerous ground. Ed Byrne will cover that ground between now and the next provincial campaign.

But the Conservatives of 1999 will tell you their's is a different kind of party. Paul Cooper says the party has shaken off its impatient early years in opposition. They have rid themselves of three leaders after Liberal victories. Tom Rideout left after the 1989 election; Len Simms left after the 1993 vote; and Lynn Verge was practically booted out after the loss in 1996. What then, will save Ed Byrne's hide?

Paul Cooper feels part of Ed Byrne's strength is that he is the opposite of Brian Tobin's charismatic and flamboyant manner. "The smooth style is something people are a little tired of right now, it is tiring and will wear itself out over the next little while," he says. "Ed comes across as being sincere and articulate and common."

There may be something else that will play in Ed Byrne's favour, as long as he does not commit big mistakes. The present elected members of the party are without any significant ties to the Peckford and Moores eras. That allows Ed Byrne to claim he has independence of thought, and perhaps most important, he can disavow himself and his party of their association with the last, wasteful days of Conservative power. There is a powerful symbolism in a party under Ed Byrne paying off the last campaign debt from the Peckford era.

Ed Byrne accomplished something in the 1999 campaign, that he could not have achieved without running an election as leader — he gained a profile. "We watched Ed grow," says his close friend and assistant Kim Puddister.

Loyola Hearn, who was courted by Byrne to head his office as chief of staff, says "it's no longer — 'who is Ed Byrne?' — the Ed Byrne of today is a lot more mature and polished than the Ed Byrne of six months ago." Hearn contends Byrne will be there as leader for the next election, "unless he doesn't want it, and there's no sign of that."

There remains just one Conservative MHA with links to the Peckford era. Tom Rideout used to be a Liberal, but just after Peckford came to power, the MHA from the then-district of Baie Verte-White Bay crossed the floor to the Conservatives. He liked Brian Peckford's style and the government's commitment to rural Newfoundland. Rideout succeeded Peckford as party leader in 1989 and for forty brief days, he was the province's fourth premier. The subsequent election showed the Clyde Wells' Liberals better prepared and better organized than the Conservatives. Perhaps seventeen years in power had made the Conservatives fat and complacent, or they may have misjudged early enthusiasm for Rideout as strong support for the party. Regardless, voters turfed the party out of office. Tom Rideout's time as premier is more a political asterisk than an accomplishment, causing Liberals and some Conservatives to question his return to the backbench when he could be practicing law with his recently-earned law degree, and drawing on his nearly $60,000 provincial pension.

Paul Cooper, who lost to John Efford in Port de Grave, ponders the Rideout question. "It's a mystery," he says of Rideout's return to politics, "that someone could become so motivated to work for less than he makes not working [drawing on his pension] and if he was working with his law practice." But Cooper says he takes Rideout at his word that politics is in his blood and he wanted to stay involved. But Cooper, who at 40, considers himself as part of "the backbone of the party," claims there is no room in the party for people with ulterior motives. "There's no room in the party for Tom Rideout to become leader. That day is past, it is long past," he says.

Jack Harris and the New Democrats do not appear to play the same games of political intrigue as the Liberals and Conservatives. Until the 1999 election, Harris *was* the NDP caucus in the House. Having gained a seat, the party has potential for a higher profile. And its strong finish in Atlantic Canada, especially in Nova Scotia in the 1997 federal election, showed there was a receptive audience for the party and its position on Atlantic Canadian issues. But the Nova Scotia breakthrough did not spread to Newfoundland, where voters appear content to switch their allegiance back and forth between the Liberals and Conservatives. And in Newfoundland in 1985, the New Democrats polled close to 15-percent of the vote and then slid backwards in subsequent elections. The challenge for Jack Harris, if he is to see the party grow in Newfoundland, is to capitalize on discontent about social issues and spread a vision of government that is palatable to voters. And in order to do that, he has to show evidence that the NDP is a real contender for power in Newfoundland politics.

Despite the opportunities and pitfalls that face the Conservatives and New Democrats, the political landscape in Newfoundland and Labrador remains dominated by Brian Tobin. He is still the focus of political discourse. Some believe he dug his own political grave when he legislated an end to the nurses' strike. Yet, political events have a way of fading from public memory. Angry confrontations and threats have a way of dissipating over time. On the potentially positive side of the ledger, people will watch closely to assess Brian Tobin's handling of Voisey's Bay and Churchill Falls. His promise to parley good deals on those two major resource issues into a "psychological departure point" for Newfoundlanders is a mighty challenge. Tobin feels Newfoundlanders as a people are so accustomed to things going wrong that they are pessimistic about any kind of development prospect. If Newfoundland can get a good deal on one or both of Churchill Falls or Voisey's Bay, Tobin believes that will become the "departure point" from a past that is remembered more for its failures than its successes.

Then, there is the rest of Brian Tobin's life. He is in his mid-40's and his children have grown up in political life. He spends more time away from his wife and family than he would like. In our meeting in his office on a sunny September morning, he talked of writing a book someday, detailing his life inside politics. He reckons the part about the 1995 turbot war with Spain would make good reading.

I have heard all the answers about his supposed ambitions to be prime minister and reported on them many times. But I need to bring the topic up for the record, in order to complete this book. I get his well-rehearsed answer, that he gets a chuckle out of the speculation on the part of journalists and pundits that he would one day like to be Prime Minister. "I tell them there's no job open," he says. I ask him if he leads journalists on by showing off his French from time to time. Right on cue, he answers in French, saying it's important in a country like Canada for a Premier to be able to speak Canada's two official languages. Then he gets serious. "Jean Chretien suggests he's staying on. If he's running for a third term, then the only thing I can do is focus on my second term. At the end of the second term, I can take stock and prepare for my succession in the Liberal Party or prepare to run another term. If there's an opening then federally, I will take a look at it."

There's one final point to be made as Tobin shows me to the door. "Have you seen the latest issue of *l'Actualite* [the French equivalent of Maclean's]?," he wants to know. The cover story is by journalist Michel Vastel and in it, he claims Chretien is intent on staying for one more election. If that happens, the scenario for a successor to Chretien may change. Paul Martin, the Finance Minister and acknowledged front-runner to replace Chretien, may be out of the running because people could perceive a mid-60's politician too old to embark on his first term as Prime Minister.

There is a cartoon Tobin draws my attention to in the Vastel article — an aging and perspiring Paul Martin is being chased by a young schoolboy look-alike in shorts, Brian Tobin. It is a moment Tobin enjoys. I can't tell if it's because of the absurdity of such a notion or if it's because he's anticipating another race, the run of his life.

Epilogue

Some of the people I introduced in this book achieved their political objectives, some did not. What follows is a brief description of what they were doing in the fall of 1999.

Randy Collins was elected MHA for Labrador West by a 156-vote margin.

Perry Canning is now Executive Director of Corporate Development in the provincial Department of Industry Trade and Technology. In the summer of 1999, Canning sold his home and cottage in Labrador City and moved to Mount Pearl.

Yvonne Jones won Cartwright-L'anse au Clair with the highest percentage of the popular vote in the province — 84.74%.

Paul Cooper polled just over 1000 votes. He's operating his landscaping business, Colorstone Interlockers.

John Efford was reappointed Minister of Fisheries and Aquaculture.

Paul Dicks was reappointed Minister of Finance.

Kevin Aylward was reappointed Minister of Forest Resources and Agrifoods.

Joan Marie Aylward won her seat by 166 votes and was reappointed Minister of Health.

Lloyd Matthews won by 333 votes and was reappointed Minister of Municipal and Provincial Affairs.

Tom Hedderson won Harbour Main-Whitbourne by more than a thousand votes and is the Conservative critic on education.

Paul Shelley was reelected in Baie Verte.

George Furey, the Liberal campaign manager, was appointed by the Prime Minister to the Senate.

Malcolm Rowe, the province's top-ranking civil servant, was appointed to the Supreme Court of Newfoundland.

There are many more names that could be added to this list, people who contibuted in a large way to helping me understand the "real" election campaign. Many of them are in sensitive political positions and do not wish to be identified. Others enjoy private life outside politics, and also wish to remain anonymous. To all these people, and those who have allowed me to quote them directly, my deepest thanks. Politics is too important a part of our lives to remain the exclusive domain of the few. I hope that this book, in some small way, will expand our understanding of the way Newfoundland elections are run.

Some of the policy issues discussed during the election, have taken a new turn since. Despite Paul Dicks spirited attack on the Conservatives' plan to reduce taxes, the Liberals themselves appointed a committee to look into such a matter.

On the Voisey's Bay issue, Mines and Energy Minister Roger Grimes told *Here & Now* the province *may* consider allowing INCO to ship out unprocessed ore, if it remains committed to building a mine and smelter in Newfoundland.

Index